T0137697

LIFE

AND

ADVENTURES

ON

MISSION TRIPS

Dr. Spencer Meckstroth

Order this book online at www.trafford.com
or email orders@trafford.com

Most Trafford titles are also available at major online book retailers.

Printed in the United States of America.

ISBN: 978-1-4269-5405-4 (sc)
ISBN: 978-1-4269-5406-1 (hc)
ISBN: 978-1-4269-5407-8 (e)

Library of Congress Control Number: 2011900179

Trafford rev. 06/09/2011

 www.trafford.com

North America & international
toll-free: 1 888 232 4444 (USA & Canada)
phone: 250 383 6864 ♦ fax: 812 355 4082

About the Author

Spencer Meckstroth is the son of an Indiana pastor. He was the vice president of his senior class at Bluffton high school and captain of the basketball team. He graduated from the Ohio State Optometry School.

Spencer and his wife, Ann, have three children and seven grandchildren. Both sons are medical doctors and their daughter is a high school English teacher. They also raised a niece from age 10. She is a beautician. and has three children and eight grandchildren.

Spencer was an optometrist in Louisville, Ohio for ten years, before moving to West Palm Beach, Florida, where he was an optometrist for over thirty years, before retiring. He has taught Sunday School for many years.

In 1989 Spencer went on his first medical mission trip, using his skills as an optometrist.
By now, in 2010, Spencer has been on over 80 short term mission trips to 23 countries.

In some respects, the medical needs for doctors, dentists, optometrists and nurses is very great and much the same in all these underprivileged countries visited. But frequently, different problems or circumstances come up, requiring an adjustment or change in plans Spencer has learned that missionaries need to be flexible.

Spencer has had several articles published in optometric periodicals and in newspapers, and he has written several books which have not yet been published. This is his first published book. Enclosed in it is a poem he wrote to his fiancee many years ago.

Acknowledgements

Nobody writes a book by himself. Although one person may type the words into his computer, there are countless others who contribute in a less noticeable manner. I wish to thank the following who have helped me with this book.

Willie Howe, with whom my wife and I had a group Bible study for 20 years, who went on a mission trip with us, and who wrote a chapter about her trip with us to Venezuela. She also proofread this entire book, which was of immeasurable help.

Alfred Vazquez, my nephew, who installed a new computer for me and rescued me from various computer jams and odd glitches.

Jordan Alessi, my grandson, who installed a new monitor when my old one suddenly quit on me and helped when my computer jammed or would not do what I wanted it to do.

My daughter, Janet Alessi, who helped to organize this book and who used her skill as an English teacher to proofread the text, give me helpful suggestions on revisions, and helped me to express my message better.

My son, Clyde, who has gone on mission trips with me, encourages me, helps with my computer, and helps in various other ways.

Team members, who have proofread chapters about their trips and have corrected any errors or omissions they noticed.

All of the various churches, groups, or individuals that have invited me to partner with them on a mission trip Each trip has been special, and each has had its own unique story.

And last, but not least, my wife Anna, who encouraged me to finish this book when I was discouraged and tired. She is the joy of my life and has honored me by making me a father three times.

Various authors write books for different reasons. I find the subject of short term mission trips so interesting that I feel that I must share the joys of my experiences.

The purpose of this book is to tell you the story about my short term mission trips in such a way that hopefully you will be encouraged to go on such a trip yourself in the near future. Then you will get a good taste of missions.

Introduction

Christ stood on a mountaintop in Galilee, almost 2000 years ago, and gave his final instructions to his disciples as recorded in Matthew 28: "Go therefore and make disciples of all nations, baptizing them in the name of the Father and of the Son and of the Holy Spirit, teaching them to observe all that I have commanded you."

Using these words, called the Great Commission, Jesus sent out his disciples. Their efforts have affected each one of us and also the entire world. When Jesus returns one of these days or years, what will he discover by watching and talking with us? Are we knowledgeable witnesses, or so poorly equipped that you could almost call us illiterate?

Recently our church videotaped our interviews with some people on the street. They were asked if they could name 10 kinds of beer. Most of them could. Then they were asked if they could name the 10 commandments. Most of the people could only name three or four, and a few could name five or six. Most of them denied breaking any of the 10 commandments, except after very pointed cross-examination. Some of these people claimed that they went to church sometimes. It doesn't seem that they had learned much, as they were rather Biblically illiterate.

During another interview, people were asked to name 10 kinds of cigarettes. Most could. Next, they were asked to name Christ's 12 disciples. Few could name more than three or four.

After three years of watching and listening to Christ's teaching, preaching, and healing, the 12 disciples were expected to be ready to teach others the gospel, who would mature and then in turn, teach other people the gospel. The cycle would repeat itself over and over.

Who sent out the first preaching team-medical mission team? Jesus Christ Himself, almost 2,000 years ago. (Read Matthew 9:35-38; Matthew 10:1-15; Mark 6:7-13, 6:30; and Luke 9:1-6, 9:10.) Also, in Luke 10:17, Jesus appointed 70 more disciples and sent them out.

They preached that the Kingdom of Heaven was at hand, and Jesus empowered them to heal the sick and lame. (These were the first medical mission trips.)

Jesus instructed his 12 disciples to go in pairs only to the Jews, but not to the Gentiles or to Samaritans. Evidently, Jesus realized that at first the disciples needed to get experience and confidence working with people from their own country and using their own language. Jesus knew they were not yet equipped to take His message to all the world.

Upon His departure, a year or two later, Jesus would command the disciples to take the same message to all the nations in the world. Many spoke different languages. Perhaps this first short-term preaching/medical trip only lasted a week or two or three, but it prepared the disciples for their trips in the future.

Today, if we are to witness to others, we need to know the basic doctrines of Christianity and exactly what we believe. Christians 2,000 years ago often knew Jesus personally or knew someone who knew Him or had seen Him. Today, we have the benefits of 2,000 years of history, missionary efforts, creeds, revivals,...etc, and we have the Bible to study.

But do we study the Bible daily? Do we read the Sunday school lesson before class? Do we take notes on the sermon as we listen to our preacher in church, and then search out the Scriptures to see if he has spoken the truth? They did so in Berea when Paul preached there in ancient times (Acts 17:11).

If we have not witnessed to others around our hometown, we need to gain experience in doing that before going on a mission trip without any practice. (Even sports teams practice often before the season starts.)

Now let me make myself clear: only Jesus can heal instantly and completely without any limitations.

Medical, dental, and eye care have made tremendous advances in the last 2,000 years, especially the last 100 years.

Modern medicines and surgery, dental care, glasses, and eye surgery can cure or control diseases and conditions that were non-curable in ancient times. For example, leprosy and trachoma can be controlled, and cataracts can be operated on today.

We need to use the best medical care available. When a mission team goes to a town where medical care is non-existent or far behind the times, our mission doctors distribute medicines that help tremendously in a few days. Glasses make these people see better instantly. This seems like a miracle to them.

Often good medical care is not available to them, or else if it is, they simply can not afford it. Often there is another problem present: what a man earns today is what his family buys food with for tomorrow. If he takes a day or two or three off to go to the doctor, then his family will have no food to eat for those days. For example, if it takes a man one day to travel to the doctor, another day to see the doctor and have tests, and then another day to travel home, his income is lost-- his family will starve for those three days.

**

This brings out the importance of doing what we can to take FREE help to those in need.

Once they have seen Christ in action through the medical missionaries sent to them, hopefully they will want to know more about Him!

**

Anyone leaving on a short term mission trip should remember what Jesus said in Matthew 25:40: "In as much as you have done it unto one of the least of these my brethren, you have done it unto Me." That's a good motto for any mission trip. Those that read this book may be taking their first steps towards going on a mission trip. You may turn your "someday" dream into reality!

This book is not a theoretical book on techniques or methods to be used in witnessing on mission trips. It is not a guide on how to choose a mission team, or a way to choose the destination for your trip.

It is a summation of interesting incidents and events that occur on mission trips.

Table of Contents

Note: All Scripture quotations are from the King James Version of the Bible.

Chapter 1: Who Took the Most Important Short-Term Mission Trip?

Who went on the most important short term mission trip? God sent his only son Jesus, on a short term mission trip to the Earth, with a special purpose to accomplish: to redeem the world. Jesus fulfilled hundreds of prophesies. After he died on the cross, rose from the dead, and trained his disciples, then his task on earth was finished. Just before He returned to heaven, Jesus said to His disciples, "You are to go into all the world and preach the Good News to everyone, everywhere" (Mark 16:15). You and I are included in this group.

Another important early mission or trip occurred when the wickedness of man was so great that God decided to destroy mankind with a great flood. However Noah, a just man, found favor in God's eyes and was commissioned to build a huge ark to save mankind and two of each species of animal life. Years later, after much ridicule from his neighbors, Noah completed the Ark. He and his family and all the animals boarded the ark. The flood came and destroyed everybody and everything not in the ark, in accordance to God's plan. Mission fulfilled.

A candidate for an early special purpose mission trip would be Joseph. God escalated a series of events that caused Joseph to be sold into slavery in Egypt, and God mysteriously caused him to rise in power and become the second most powerful man in Egypt. Thus he was able to save the Jewish nation from starvation and fulfill God's plan.

At the burning bush, God chose Moses, at age 80, to lead the Israelites out of Egypt. Moses is known as a friend of God. In accordance with God's plan, Moses delivered them from Egypt and led them to the Red Sea, where God dramatically opened a path across for them to escape the Egyptians. He led them through the 40 years in the desert, and went up Mount Sinai to receive the Ten Commandments.. He wrote the first five books of the Bible. He led them to the edge of Palestine. Mission accomplished. He was a great leader.

A candidate for an early special purpose mission successfully completed would be Esther. God selected her to become Queen of Media-Persia. Her efforts canceled the efforts of Prime Minister Haman, the second most powerful man in that kingdom, to have all the Jews exterminated. That would have prevented many of the prophesies about Jesus from being fulfilled and would have prevented his Jewish birth. She helped God fulfill His plans.

Two other people, Mary the mother of Jesus, and Joseph his earthly father, are two people with great faith in God. They trusted Him completely. They literally had their lives changed entirely when they agreed to God's plan for their lives of having and raising Jesus. Imagine all the ridicule and shame they had to endure at first, and the insults, etc. that would follow for years to come. But they persevered without complaint and did as the Lord led them. They accomplished their God-given special purpose mission.

The Apostle Paul was an enemy of the Christians before his life changing Damascus Road experience, but he went on many short term mission trips for the Lord all over the then known world. He may not have been the first, but he was definitely one of the best and most traveled. He wrote 13 books of the New Testament, and possibly Hebrews also. The last half of the book of Acts is about Paul. He spread the Gospel throughout the then known world..

In Romans 8:28, we read that "God causes all things to work together for good to those who love God, to those who are called according to his purpose." We can see the truth in that verse in all six cases mentioned above, of people called for a special purpose mission.

**

What are the reasons for the recent proliferation of short term mission trips today?

Obviously the jet airplane, telephones, cell phones, email, the Internet, credit cards, microphones, audio/loud speaking systems, trucks, automobiles, buses, new restaurants and hotels, etc. are big factors in this expansion. Before that, the printing press, copying machines, and Bible translation teams.

**

My challenge to you and to each and every person that reads this book is that you will be inspired to make these resolutions:

(1) I will try to be a witness for the Lord each day.
(2) I will go on a short term mission trip each year.
(3) If I am physically unable to go, I will generously donate money to my church so that someone else may go in my place. I will also pray for that someone while on this trip.

**

"Therefore said He unto them. The harvest truly is great, but the labourers are few: pray ye therefore the Lord of the harvest, that He would send forth labourers into His harvest" (Luke 10:2).

**

3

"Go ye therefore, and teach all nations, baptizing them in the name of the Father, and of the Son, and of the Holy Ghost. Teaching them to observe all things whatsoever I have commanded you: and lo I am with you always, even unto the end of the world. Amen" (Matthew 28 19-20).

**

We need to spend as much time as possible in our home towns, telling our children, families, friends, co-workers, and neighbors about Jesus. We should not be lukewarm Christians for 50-52 weeks a year and then be a red hot Christian for one or two weeks a year while we are on a mission trip. Quit pretending. Be a full time Christian.

**

Martin Luther said, "A Christian shoemaker does not do his duty by putting little crosses on shoes, but by making good shoes. He is known by his work. This satisfies both his employer and the person who buys the shoes."

**

We read in Romans 10:15, "How beautiful are the feet of them that preach the Gospel of peace and bring glad tidings of good things." How true this is. Let these feet be yours.

**

Today, when many people go on a mission trip, they really wish to walk in the footsteps of Jesus. Not necessarily literally in Israel , but figuratively in a foreign country--doing what Jesus did every day during his ministry.

Jesus has commanded us to spread the Good News to the far ends of the earth. To do so on mission trips, we give out Bibles and New

Testaments in their language, treat their sick, blind and injured, give them food and clothing, talk to them through translators, hug them and sing with them, we are friends to them, and we serve them in any other way we can.

**

We read about all the different things Jesus did and then try to emulate Jesus and do those same things, all with the love of Jesus in our hearts. This is probably as close as we can come to being Christ like and walking in the footsteps of Jesus.

**

Some people come back from a mission trip with their eyes opened and with a drastically different viewpoint on what it is to be Christ like. My question to you is, "What difference did/or will this mission trip make in your life?"

**

In Oct. 1992, my optician son-in-law Greg, went with our group of 15-16 optometrists and opticians on a mission trip to Homestead, Fl. shortly after Hurricane Andrew. One optometrist had a 50 ft RV converted into a mobile optometrist office, with an optical lab. We all traveled in it. This RV plus an adjacent large 60x60ft tent served as our clinic.

For those who had lost their homes and glasses during the hurricane, our mission was to replace their glasses so that they could see to work and read again.

We examined their eyes for disease and checked for glasses. If needed, our lab made them glasses within an hour, or ordered bifocals if needed, to be delivered within a few days. Hundreds of people were so grateful to be able to see again.

Nearby, other organizationas were giving out free clothing, food and water, and supplies.

**

My wife Ann has been on nine medical mission trips with me: to the Turks and Caicos twice and to the Dominican Republic, Trinidad, Mexico, Venezuela, Honduras twice, & Paraguay. She is my Spanish translator and makes my trips so much more interesting.

**

My oldest son Clyde is a medical doctor, and we have been together on two medical mission trips: to Brazil and to India.

**

My grandson, Jordan, age 20, has been on two youth mission trips in the USA with our church, and in June 2009, he and I were on a multi faceted trip to Costa Rica.

**

After the flood, and when all the people and animals had left the Ark, finally Noah and his wife left too. As they walked away, Noah's wife looked back for one last look, and she turned to Noah and said, " Noah, we can't leave the Ark here like this. It will be a terrible eyesore to this whole area." Noah smiled at her and said, "Don't worry, dear, I left the termites on board."(JOKE)

**

Chapter 2: Have Glasses--Will Travel

I am a retired optometrist who has dedicated the past 22 years of my life to going on short term mission trips to various countries around the world.

I have been privileged to travel on over 80 such trips to 23 different countries, on five continents. Living in West Palm Beach, Florida, has provided me with proximity to the airports of Miami, Fort Lauderdale, and West Palm Beach, which has been advantageous for my many trips. While I was working, I could work in the office in the morning and then leave to catch an afternoon flight in Miami, 60 miles away. This way I only missed a half day's work before and after each trip, which was quite beneficial. Since many of these trips were before 9/11, I didn't have to check in two hours early.

This book is a collection of over 200 incidents, illustrations, events, facts, and short stories, some humorous, some inspiring, some exciting, and some pathetic or sad, about my experiences with the people of various countries over the years. Several of the people who have inspired and influenced me are mentioned also.

My first medical mission trip was in 1989. It was a trip to Belize (formerly called British Honduras) in central America.

Besides helping the people of Belize, the main purpose of this trip was to prepare me for the problems and conditions that I would encounter on my next trip, about seven or eight weeks later, to the Amazon River in Brazil. I wanted to be a good Boy Scout and "Be Prepared."

I traveled with Reverend Glen and Marie Ross, former missionaries to Belize. They had the personal connections in Belize to have everything set up in advance: housing, food, transportation and publicity announcements made several weeks before we arrived, at the various churches where we could hold our clinics. I found out what strengths of glasses I would need, what kind of equipment to bring, and the conditions I would work under. It was a good trip. It just stirred my heart when I would see someone come forward and accept the Lord. They got glasses they could see with, and all who could read were given New Testaments or gospel literature in Spanish or English, whichever they preferred. Mission accomplished.

**

After my first trip to Belize, some people in Belize made a special request to the missionaries I had worked with, that when I return to Belize, that I go to their town and hold an eye clinic as I had in several neighboring towns. They needed glasses too. Ask and ye shall receive. They got their wish.

**

Free medical clinics such as these are often held in churches. The purpose of the medical team is to attract their underprivileged people into a local church where they are given free medical, dental, and eye care, glasses and medicines. They are also given Bibles, New Testaments, and literature in their language, and witnessed to by Christians from their own country.

Most of these people would never enter that church except for their extreme desire and need for medical care. They see our love for Christ and our love for them by our willingness to take time out of our lives to travel to their country to help them. Local missionaries and pastors there say that this function is extremely important to them.

A list of all the patients seen and what was done for them, is given to the missionaries or local pastors so they can follow up on each person. If they meet them on the street, the pastor can ask them, "How is your knee doing?" or "How are you seeing with your new glasses?" or "How are your teeth?" etc.

**

I've never gotten over the thrill of having a native patient put on his new glasses. First there is a long drawn-out, "Aaaaaaah!" Then I listen as they joyfully exclaim, "Now I can see again! Now I can see again!" They look around the room excitedly, and with a smile a mile wide on their face, exclaim, "I haven't been able to see like this for years." Then I know that I have made a difference in their lives forever.

**

To read the Bible, a person has to have one. That is why we always like to give out Bibles or New Testaments in a person's own language to the people we visit.

**

The age of 40 is of particular significance in the eyecare profession. Up until age 40, many people do not need eyeglasses to see, to read, or to sew. But when people reach age 40, often their near vision goes downhill rapidly, and they soon need reading glasses or bifocals.

Some people have that problem before they reach 40, but not a large percentage.

In many countries, where people do not have a proper nutritious diet, and do not have proper lighting for reading or sewing, many of the people often develop reading problems several years earlier. Often these people do tedious work which requires good "near vision," such as sewing, weaving, pottery, painting, carving, etc., often straining their eyes under very poor lighting such as candlelight or kerosene lights or firelight. This just aggravates their eye problems even more.

This is why eye care and glasses given out on short term mission trips, is so important for many people in the world who can't afford proper care, or have no eyecare facilities available. They are given back their eyesight and can work again. They usually are quite astonished at how well they can see again. They do not have to be beggars anymore. Often they are highly skilled craftsmen.

**

Dr. Meckstroth spent a week in Belize in 1989. After working in Belize City, Sand Hill, and Orange Walk, he held clinics in two churches in the seaport city of Corozal in northern Belize. There he met and examined Lydia and Carlos.

Fourteen year old Lydia was a cute teenager, but her future did not look too bright. She had dropped out of school because she could not see well enough to do her school work. She liked school, but she just couldn't see the black board. She lived with her mother in an abandoned store shanty which had been finished with discarded scrap lumber wired together and sealing cracks with dried clay. They had thatched the roof themselves with palm fronds. She had to walk within four feet of the E-chart to read the small letters. She worked long hours in a Chinese laundry washing clothes. It didn't pay much, and it had no future, but at least it was a job.

Ten year old Carlos was a beggar boy. He had been born with his right eye extremely far sighted, and his left eye almost blind. Carlos had struggled with his school work and did so poorly on exams, that his teachers recommended he stay home. He was a beggar now and seemed destined to be a beggar the rest of his life. He lived in a stick and dried clay house with his parents. It had a rusty old metal roof which his father had pitched in several places to stop the leaks. His father was a part time sugar cane cutter and did odd jobs when he could find work. Carlos could barely see the big *E* on the E-chart.

When Lydia tried on her highly nearsighted glasses, she just shouted for joy in her excited thrill of being able to see it all clearly now. She promised to go back to school. When Carlos tried on his very strong farsighted glasses, he just looked around the room, shaking his head in amazement at how clearly he saw. Finally he broke down and started crying in happiness. Carlos is going back to school also.

These used glasses made a world of difference to these two children. The glasses are literally changing their lives. Over 600 more Belizean children and adults were fit that week, and their lives were also changed dramatically.

**

I've been taking used glasses to Third World countries for over 22 years, helping restore sight to poverty stricken children and adults. It is easy for any optometrist like me to test their eyes and give them glasses. However, the most time consuming part of this type of mission work is

(1) collecting enough glasses,
(2) cleaning them and discarding broken or badly scratched pairs, and
(3) sorting and marking glasses by prescription power

This is difficult for a busy full-time optometrist with a wife and family competing for his time.

**

After I had made my first two trips, I submitted stories of my trips to the local newspapers. Soon churches, clubs, schools, and senior citizen groups started calling and asking me to speak to their organization. Instead of an honorarium, often these groups would collect a couple boxes of used glasses to help for my next trip.

I spoke to several Lions Clubs, and after my second talk to the West Palm Beach Lions club, they made me an honorary member for all my humanitarian work. This news quickly spread to other Lions clubs in the district, and soon I was receiving 500-600 pairs of glasses at a time. I even got glasses from Lions clubs in other states. Several funeral homes called me up about twice a year and told me they had a bunch of glasses for me to stop by and pick up.

I talked to the WPB Rotary club, and a visiting Rotarian from the Cayman Islands heard me and sent me over 500 pairs which he had received from England. Several other local Rotarians collected hundreds of glasses for mission work also.

**

I have received glasses from many states, and sometimes from people I don't even know. There usually is a note inside, telling me that a certain person told the sender about me and that the sender approved of my humanitarian work and wished to donate some glasses he had collected for distribution in developing countries.

By this time, I was averaging four trips a year for 19 years, and so I needed a large supply of glasses. Some boxes of donated used glasses are half full of unusable, broken, or cracked frames--frames with broken lenses, with one lens missing, or with broken temples, etc.

Other boxes have obviously had all the trash culled out. They have even been cleaned and are a delight to receive. Occasionally, a box comes in with the powers already marked, and these are especially wonderful to receive.

Before I retired, the optician at my office was my son in law Greg, who helped me prepare many pairs of glasses for my trips. Every so often, my wife, Ann, and I would have a marking party and mark several hundred pairs a night. It helped that I have a lens meter at home.

At my office there was a box for people to donate their old glasses for the needy, when they got a new pair of glasses. One lady donated her old but very expensive glasses and made this comment: "I just wish I could see who got my glasses." So I specially marked her glasses and then took a picture of the recipient of her glasses, and when I returned, I gave the picture to the lady who had donated the glasses.. She was delighted.

**

Retired now, I use the digital lens meter at my former office, which makes it easier and faster to verify the power of the lenses

**

I'm sure that many people who read this book never imagined that donated glasses could make such a difference, but they can change a person's life.

Helen Keller addressed the worldwide delegates at the International Lions Convention in 1925, and as a result of her speech, the Lions

Clubs adopted the primary mission of aiding the visually impaired. What a speech that must have been, from such a great lady.

I'll share a famous quotation from Helen Keller: "There is no better way to thank God for your sight than by giving a helping hand to someone in the dark."

A variation of this quotation is, "There is no better way to thank God for your salvation, than by telling someone in the dark about salvation, about your experience."

**

Tracoma is the leading cause of preventable blindness in developing countries, especially in dry arid regions. It is endemic in North Africa, Middle East, India, southeast Asia, but rarely in the USA or in northern Europe. Often it is due to sexual transmission, poor sanitation or crowded living conditions. Early signs are a whitish haze coming down into the pupil from above, followed by blood vessel infiltration. Modern medicines and treatment can clear it, if started in time.

**

Also, pterygiums are often seen on mission trips. This fleshy white growth usually grows from the nasal part of eye towards the pupil and is due to exposure to unprotected ultra violet sunlight and / or irritation from rubbing dry, dusty eyes. Constant use of UV sunglasses often prevents this, and simple surgery can eliminate it.

**

PROBLEM?--When our medical mission team comes to town, the eye clinic checks eyes and gives out free glasses to everyone needing glasses. Soon it becomes popular and stylish to have glasses. It gives them a certain amount of prestige and something to talk about. Soon many people want free glasses, even if they do not need them.

This is especially true for children. They lie, and pretend they can not see very well.

SOLUTION: If the town has electricity, do an auto refractor test which gives a very good idea of what their prescription is.

If no auto refractor is available, check each eye for acuity, then refract eye for power.

Have several nice looking pairs of plano clear glasses nearby. If you suspect malingering or lying about their vision, use them.. They are an excellent diagnostic tool.

When you have reached their best prescription, try several pair of glasses on them, including a pair of plano glasses. If they say this plano pair is much better, have them read the bottom line. If they can, you know they are lying. Tell them that these are just play glasses with no power, and they do not need glasses. They sheepishly know that you have caught them in their lie, and will turn away and leave. Seldom will they argue.

Spencer Checking Little Girl's Eyes

15

Chapter 3: Impressions of a "First-Timer"--Venezuela

What a privilege it was to be invited by Spencer and Ann Meckstroth to accompany them on one of their mission trips. Our destination was Valencia, Venezuela, and the date was May 2001.

Our 20+ group consisted of a construction crew to help build an addition to a church, a Bible School group for the children, and the eye clinic. We were hosted by missionaries Reverend and Mrs. Leon Champion and Reverend and Mrs. Ted Lott. This was my first mission trip.

My first impression of Venezuela was that it is a beautiful country, mild in temperature, even though it was May, and close to the equator. The elevation and pleasant breeze kept it very comfortable. However, the presence of military all over the place reminded us we were not in paradise. Even the entrance to the hotel where we stayed was heavily guarded.

My impression of the people was that they are very pleasant and charming, truly happy to have us there. The children that came for the Bible school were neat, clean, and well-mannered. Since all grades share the same school, the young ones attended in the morning, and the older ones in the afternoon. Thus, the little ones were able to attend Bible school in the afternoon.

When we arrived each morning at the church where Spencer would be conducting eye exams, there were *many* people sitting on chairs awaiting our arrival, all smiles when they saw us, anticipating receiving the gift of better vision.

Spencer patiently examined each patient, first with an ophthalmoscope for disease, then using the E-chart to estimate what power was needed, and then trying on different glasses (each marked with the prescription) until the correct lenses were found. Of course Ann was a huge help since she was by his side translating. When the correct glasses were found, Ann handed the glasses to me. I removed the markings, slipped them into an eyeglass case, and handed them to the patient. In response, I got *besos* (kisses).

What a joy it was to see these people, so loving and so appreciative. I remember the case of a 13-year-old boy whose vision was so bad that none of the glasses we had would help him. Spencer accompanied him into town for an appointment with a doctor who could provide the help he needed. Spencer personally paid for the cost of this visit.

Our last evening there, a worship service was held.. What a *joy* that was! The Holy Spirit knows no language barrier! We were one in the Spirit, and we praised our God together. Especially impressive was a group of teen-agers and their praise pantomime skit which they performed.

Anyone who has an experience in missions wants to go back. This was the case with me for sure. In fact, I made tentative plans to return on my own and assist with their ministry. However, political unrest made it unwise to make the trip. I'll end this as I began it: What a privilege!

Chapter 4: Easter Sunrise Service on Top of Pyramid in Belize

On a medical mission trip a number of years ago, we were in Belize for a long week, including the Easter weekend. Several days before Easter, our pastor, Reverend Ross, recommended that we hold an Easter sunrise service on top of a large tall, pyramid at the Altun Ha Maya park, which had perhaps seven or eight pyramids that we had visited before.

"Yes," we readily agreed, "that would be nice." We had all been to various places for a sunrise service, but none of us had been on *top* of a pyramid for an Easter sunrise service. As a matter of fact, we had never heard of anyone who had attended such a service.

Sunrise was at 5:45am, so we set our alarm clocks for 4:00am. We all got up somewhat sleepy, but eager to go.. By 5:00am all 12 of us were driving away in a car and a van. It was very dark, with only a quarter moon and starlight by which to see. We all wore light jackets to ward off the cool morning breeze. We each used our flashlights as we walked from the parking area to the pyramids. Upon reaching the base of the tallest one, one after the other, we started climbing the steps to the top. By the time we got to the top, all of us were winded and almost out of breath.

Looking around in the starlight and the faint moonlight, we could see that we were above the treetops of the various trees surrounding the pyramid park. The silhouettes of the treetops were softly fluttering in the early morning breeze. Off to the south, we could see the lights from Belize City, the capitol, but they were not as bright as some American cities at night.

Looking towards the eastern horizon we could see a brighter area, indicating where the sun would be peeping up soon. One of the men played a harmonica, and he was our accompanist as we sang "He Arose," "He Lives," and "The Old Rugged Cross."

Reverend Ross led us in prayer and began talking about the significance of Easter As we all listened, we watched in awe as the sunrise took place before our wonder-filled eyes. It was interesting to behold how, for a short period of time, darkness seemed to wrestle with the light until at last the sun burst over the horizon and finally darkness vanished. The creation of the world took place millions of years ago, just like this sunrise created a new day for us to enjoy and to tell others about the God who created this planet we call our earthen home. The kaleidoscopic whirl of brilliant orange colors at sunrise illustrates the power and glory of our omnipresent Lord. When the rising sun at dawn rested about two feet above the distant horizon to the east, and we were humbled by the magnificent sunrise, we silently filed down the pyramid after an Easter sunrise experience we would never forget. It was easier going down the pyramid than it had been climbing up.

**

Many years ago, I was on my second medical mission trip to Belize. As usual, there was a long line of people waiting to see me. When an elderly man's turn came, I asked, "What is the problem with your eyes?" He replied, "I had cataract surgery on both eyes several years ago, but now I see worse than I did before the surgery." I looked closely at his eyes to see if there was any corneal scarring. They looked fine. Then I checked the retinas inside both eyes with my ophthalmoscope, and they looked normal, too. Then I asked him, "Do you have any glasses?" "No" he replied, "I never had any. Now when I hear that someone is going to have cataract surgery, I tell him not to. I see much worse after my cataract surgery than I did before the surgery." I covered his right eye and turned on the scope. "Can you see this light?" I asked. "Yes," he replied. "I can see it." I then covered his left eye and turned on the scope. "Can you see the light with this eye?" I asked. "Yes," he answered. " I can see the light."

This was 18-20 years ago, before the advent of implant surgery for cataracts. At that time, people had to get glasses with very thick lenses in them, to see after cataract surgery.

I asked, "Didn't they tell you that you would need cataract glasses after surgery?" "No," he said. "They never said anything about glasses." So I tried a pair of thick cataract glasses on him. "Oh, boy," he said. "I can see much better like this!" I had about a dozen pair of thick cataract glasses with me, so I tried out all of them, and gave him the pair with which he saw the best.

"Thank you, Doctor," he said. "From now on, if someone is going to have cataract surgery, I will tell him to be sure and get the cataract glasses afterwards so he can see. I see so much better with my glasses." In my opinion, either his surgeon didn't tell him about the cataract glasses, or he didn't understand his surgeon or remember his surgeon telling him this.

**

A number of years ago, our church took part in a cooperative church building project in Orange Walk in north central Belize. Someone had donated the money to purchase a large lot on which to build a church. The Orange Walk congregation had big dreams and wanted a good sized church to serve all the needs of their area.

Many different teams came in from various churches in the USA and worked a week or two, building this church from the ground up. A week or two later, another team would come in and work for a week or so. So it went, with many groups participating. A number of local carpenters and church members worked also.

Our church went down there twice to help. While our construction group was working on one part of the building, I would hold my eye clinics in a different part of the building. Now they have a good sized active church--which I have been back to see--serving that area.

**

The life of a native missionary or pastor is often far from glamorous. Some live in the most isolated small villages in the world, often 25 miles or more from a sizable town with a doctor or dentist.

Elderly Maria lived in the humblest conditions without even the basics of running water or electricity. Every morning she had to carry a potty bucket down the steep river bank to empty into the nearby river. She had been praying for an outhouse for years.

In Belize City we were told about this faithful native pastor who led a Bible study in her home every day. We sent a three-man construction crew with a translator to serve her. On the outskirts of this village, Maria lived in a 14x16 foot building covered with a tin roof. No bathroom facilities were available.

Our workers had taken the plans, the needed lumber, nails, roofing and equipment, and had been instructed to build her an old fashioned one-holer outhouse. Upon its completion, Maria thanked each worker profusely and hugged him tightly in her happiness. "My birthday is two days from now," she exclaimed. "This outhouse is the best present I ever dreamed of. Thank you so much!"

This brought tears to our workers' eyes. We also gave her a dozen Spanish Bibles, and I gave her several pairs of reading glasses so that she and others could see better. For this, she tearfully thanked us again and again.

**

After completing the above mission trip to Belize, our team checked in at the airport an hour early for our return trip home. We were up on the verandah with a good viewing area to see planes landing and taking off. (Background information: Belize used to be called British Honduras because it was part of the British Commonwealth until it was granted independence. The British still kept a small detachment of soldiers and air force planes there for security reasons.)

All of a sudden, a pair of British Harrier jets arrived with a big roar. They flew in and stopped their forward motion in midair, hovering some 20-30 feet above the ground.. Rotating their engines, they settled straight down and landed. Then each revved up its engines, rose 20-30 feet straight up, turned around in midair, and took off in the same direction from which it came. They looked pretty much like typical fighter jets.

Ten minutes later, both planes were back and landed in their own unique style. Both the pilots got out and walked over to meet some VIP bigwigs. After a brief ceremony, the pilots got back into their planes and left with a big roar in their own unforgettable style.

As far as I know, this is the only plane in the world that can fly 500 miles per hour in its forward motion and yet maneuver like a helicopter and go out to rescue pilots who have crashed in a jungle area with no landing area. The plane just goes to a certain spot as directed by radio or GPS hovering just above the tree tops. By lowering a metal cable, the plane is able to pull up a downed flyer or injured people.

What a treat this was for our entire group. We appreciated the demonstration even if it was not planned for us. We just happened to be in the right place at the right time.

Note: The USAF did build a similar plane; however, it encountered certain problems and was discontinued.

**

While driving along a straight road between the towns of Orange Walk and Corozol in northern Belize, we noticed vertical metal poles planted in the ground very close to the two lane road on which we were driving. We asked our local missionary driver, "Why are all these poles or posts set up about every 200 feet and so close to the road? We've never seen that before."

He replied, "The surrounding fields are all strewn with rocks and gullies, shrubs, bushes, and small trees, not suitable at all for landing a small plane. We have a drug problem in this part of Belize. The drug smugglers used to land their small planes on these roads at night and drop off their shipment to local drug dealers here. Then they'd leave undetected. So our government and the police erected these posts or poles to prevent planes from landing. If a plane hits one of these, it will crash. Also, planes can not take off without hitting another pole. The poles are all set in a concrete base to prevent removal. The police have stopped all plane delivery or trafficking of drugs this way. Police cars patrol this area twice a day." "Ingenious!" we exclaimed.

"Yes," he replied. "The poles and the patrols have stopped the planes completely. However, they are probably delivering drugs some other way now."

**

Spencer at Pyramid in Belize

Chapter 5: Delivering a Baby on the Amazon River

My older son, Clyde, is a general surgeon. One time he and I were on the same medical mission trip to Brazil and were at a river town in the Amazon River valley. One evening, after holding clinic all day for the hundreds of people who came to see the different doctors, we were at evangelistic services.

A lady came running up to our meeting and said that a woman was trying to have a baby, but she was having trouble and needed help. "Where is the doctor?" we were asked.

The leader of our group called my son over and told him the story, so my son and I followed the lady to the woman's home. Sure enough, the baby was breached inside the woman and could not come out. Clyde reached in and turned the baby and soon the baby's head appeared and was born.

The mother was so appreciative of what my son had done for her, that she asked, "What is your first name?" When he said, "Clyde," she smiled. "I'm going to name my son after you," she said. "You saved my life and my son's life." So the baby was named Clyde Rodriquez in honor of Clyde.

I took several pictures of the baby, the baby and the mother, and of Clyde and the baby and the mother. Clyde has often said that he would like to go back to that town and see if his little name sake is still living. In many of those very poor areas, many of the children die before they reach the age of 2 or 3 because of disease, fevers, drinking contaminated water, malnutrition, lack of money to buy medicine,...etc.

**

On my first two trips to the Amazon river with Reverend Richard Walker and Amazon Mission Organization (AMOR), they did not own a river boat but had to rent two smaller double deck boats for groups of 28-32 people. On my first two Amazon trips, we flew in and out of Santareem, where the Tapajoz River joins the Amazon. This city is a large city about 600 miles east of Manaus

These boats were used to haul freight most of the year, and while they served the purpose, they really were not suitable for Americans. Sometimes they were smelly from a previous cargo and had to be thoroughly cleaned. First of all, one was not big enough to carry that many passengers plus a crew of 10. Secondly, they did not have enough bathrooms. Thirdly, the distance between decks was all right for the shorter Brazilians, but to be blunt, there was not enough headroom for taller Americans. I am 6'1" and I scraped my head many times. Frequently fellows 6'4" to 6'6"went on these trips, and the lack of head room really bothered them, as you might expect. Lastly, two boats use up more gas than one bigger boat, and they take two crews.

**

Therefore, AMOR started looking for a new boat. I think it was in 1991 that they found a boat that was much more ideal for them. It was larger and big enough for larger groups, had more head room between decks, had a more powerful motor which meant they could cruise faster so they could get to their destination more quickly and spend more time working there, and could be modified to meet several other needs.

The owner was very benevolent and interested in their mission work, so he offered them a very good price which they graciously accepted. The boat was named "AMOR Beatrice," in honor of Reverend Walker's wife. I have been on it for five more trips, and it is a good boat. It is a 78 foot long, double decked boat, which has served faithfully ever since. Recently they installed a new motor and did several other modifications.

**

On a typical trip today, missionaries will fly into Manaus, Brazil, which is the largest city in northern Brazil and is at the junction of two rivers which meet and form the Amazon River, the largest river in the world. From the airport they will be transferred to the boat. Depending on their arrival time, they may have a few hours to look around the city area near the harbor. If everyone is aboard and all the supplies are loaded, they will leave, sometimes at 4-5:00 p.m.

Their destination will have been pre-selected. They will travel all night, sleeping in sleeping bags on hammocks hung from the ceiling on the top deck at night, but which are tucked into the ceiling during the day. (If they simply can not sleep in a hammock, there are several foam rubber mats on which they can sleep.) The top deck will become their meeting room during the day.

The crew will sleep on the first deck, on which meals will be served by Brazilian cooks who have been trained to cook American style and cater to American tastes. They will get their food and take it up one deck to eat

27

When they arrive at their destination the next morning, their boat will pull up to the dock or pull up to shore. Everyone will go ashore. The medical team will usually go to the school, which will be closed for the duration of their stay, and which becomes their medical clinic. Rooms will be assigned to each doctor and to the pharmacy. Where the patients will wait in line will have been determined. Then the medical team will go back to the boat and help the crew members haul all the equipment and supplies to their new clinic, which they will arrange and organize.

While the medical team is doing their business, the Bible school team will go to their pre-selected building, decide how they want to arrange it, and then go back and bring their supplies to their building.

While the above two groups are getting settled in, the construction team finds out where they will work, plans what they will do, and gets ready with their supplies and equipment

By this time it is lunch time, which everyone enjoys. Then it is time for the missionaries to start doing their individual tasks. The first hour will be the hardest, as the missionaries adjust to their new schedule and working conditions. Long lines of patients will be waiting for each doctor, and by the time 10 people have been taken care of, ten more will have taken their place at the end of the line.

After dinner that evening, evangelistic services will be held. Everyone is expected to go unless he is sick. Devotions will be held every morning.

Each missionary will be told where to put his dirty clothing each morning. Each item should be marked in indelible ink with one's initials. While the missionaries are working, a Brazilian woman crew member, will wash their clothes in a washing machine, using water from the Amazon, and will hang the clothing up to dry. The clothing will be folded and ready, by dinner time or sooner.

At night time, after everyone has returned from evangelistic services, the boat will pull out from shore and go out into the middle of the river for two reasons: (1) it is usually cooler out there, and (2) there is usually a breeze that will blow away any possible mosquitoes. Usually the boat will be back at the dock when everyone awakens in the morning.

**

Each day will be about the same, with minor variations. Being in Brazil, which is just below the equator, means that during the daytime, it is often over 100 degrees Fahrenheit.

**

Many of the remote towns along the big rivers in the Amazon river valley do not have electricity during the day time. Most towns have a gasoline powered generator. Usually it only runs from 6:00-9:00 p.m. The town generator is turned off promptly at 9:00 p.m. to save gasoline. Therefore one must plan ahead and be prepared to finish his work before 9:00 p.m. or else have a lantern, candle, or flashlight ready and handy.

There is another problem that occurs occasionally. Each generator can only generate a certain amount of electricity. For example, if the generator is a 12,000 watt generator, then it can only produce enough electricity to power 300 bulbs of 40 watts each. As long as no more than 299 bulbs of 40 watts each are being used, everything is okay.

However if someone, or a couple of people plug in some extra bulbs, then the generator goes over capacity and the fuses or the circuit breakers blow, and the entire system turns off. All the lights go out; the entire town goes dark. Usually the generator operator will wait a few minutes and then restart the generator, thinking that whoever added the extra bulbs will have enough sense to turn off the extra bulbs. (Often each family is allowed only one 40 watt bulb because it costs money to pay for the gasoline to run the generator.)

If the generator starts up and works fine until the 9:00 p.m. stopping time, everything is fine. However, if it starts up and blows out almost immediately, the operator will wait a while before starting it again. This is to convince the culprits in this situation to comply with the rules.

If the operator starts the generator a third time, and it blows again, he may leave it off the rest of the evening. Of course, the various townspeople, who have been inconvenienced by not getting light as usual, will get angry with their neighbors who are overloading the system and causing the problem. Fighting may occur.

**

Sometimes we hold clinics in a town too poor to have a generator, or with a generator that has broken and has not been repaired. When we are checking the people's eyes, we ask them this question: "Do you have more of a problem seeing distance or near?" They will tell us which, but sometimes they will add, "I can see okay in the day time but can't read at night." We often find that they are trying to read by firelight, candle light, a kerosene lantern, or a propane lantern hung by the ceiling..

We tell them that in order to read or sew better at night, they should bring the lantern down and place it on the table on which they are trying to read, and they will see better. The closer the light is to what they are trying to read, the better they will see.

If they live in a town with a generator which is used at night, the same is true. The 40 watt bulb is hung from the ceiling or rafters in order to brighten the whole room.

We tell them to get a table light if possible and to put the light nearer to what they want to read or sew. If this is not possible, to get a reflector shield for the light, which will reflect all of the light down and be much better. If they live in a town where they are allowed bigger bulbs, we tell them to get a bigger one, and they will see much better.

**

If the town has a generator, we will bring the auto refractor to the eye clinic. It is a big help in accuracy and speeds up everything. If there is no town generator, and our boat is close enough, then we will run a very long extension cord from the boat's generator to the clinic at the school house for the auto refractor. Otherwise, we do without.

**

On several trips, a doctor is needed to make house calls to someone too sick or to someone crippled so badly he can not come to the clinic. When we get there, we find that it is true, they are too sick or crippled to travel. We are glad we took the time to go to this person's home to see him. We are often amazed by their living conditions. Often their home is a mud brick hut with a straw roof and dirt floors. Occasionally, they have a corrugated metal roof.

Sometimes we hear the weak sound of a baby crying. Inquiring about those sounds, we find a mother and a newborn baby. Both are too weak to travel and are starving. We give them food, liquids, baby milk, and a small blanket to keep the baby warm on cool nights, but soon we have to leave. We wonder what happens to them.

**

Clyde Delivering a Breech Baby

People Waiting in Line to See Doctors

Spencer Checking People's Eyes

Chapter 6: Alligator Hunting on the Amazon River

One day on an Amazon River medical mission trip on the AMOR riverboat, one of the crew members asked us men if we wanted to eat some alligator meat. We said, "Yes, we would like to eat some." Then he replied, "We will have to go alligator hunting tonight."

Quite skeptical, we asked the big question: "How do you do that?" He replied," Some of the men from this town where we are, know where the alligators are and will take us there tonight." We asked, "How do we get there?" He replied," We use native canoes. There will be two Brazilians and one American in each canoe."

We were even more skeptical, for we had seen many of the native canoes go by, and there were only a few inches of side board clearance above the waterline in the canoes we had seen.

During the daytime, crocodiles are practically invisible. They submerge, hide under lilies and other vegetation, logs, etc. With just their eyes above the water line, they can be watching a boat as it goes by.

When night falls, crocodiles come to life and surface to hunt and forage around like other nocturnal animals. They eat fish, anything that falls into the water, or rodents they find.

At about 9:00 p.m., away we went in four canoes. It was quite dark, with practically no moon. When we got to the right area, the canoes split up, and each silently paddled off by itself. The front man paddled slowly while the other man shone a very bright flashlight back and forth at water level, looking for two yellow eyes.

Suddenly, he whispered, "There's one."

We paddled softly toward the eyes. Considering the distance between its eyes, the man estimated its size to be three or four feet, just right for our purposes. The front man stopped paddling, reached down as we glided closer, and picked up a two-inch pipe about eight feet long.

At the right instant, he swung the pipe down on the alligator's head and killed it. I just watched. Using the hook on the end of a pole, he fished around until he found the alligator and pulled it to the boat. He tied its mouth shut, and we got our "alligator."

We ate it the next day. It tastes different but is not bad. I suppose if you didn't know what it was, it would be better. Some of our team members refused to eat it. Others liked it and had seconds. The crew members really enjoyed it. Technically, it was not an alligator, it was a Caiman, a member of the crocodile-alligator family.

**

Late one afternoon, on a medical mission to a town on the Amazon River, a messenger came and asked for a doctor and the eye doctor to come to a very sick man's home about 20 minutes away. The man had cut both feet seriously and was bleeding and couldn't walk Other villagers needed glasses.

We left 10 minutes later with two backpacks of supplies, medicines, glasses and our local guide/translators. First, we had a 10-12 minute hike along the riverside on a twisting path through the jungle to another small village, then up a small hill to the man's home. The doctor and I, both Americans, were sweating profusely when we arrived, but we were amazed at how easily our indigenous translator/ guides carrying our supplies, climbed the hill with little or no sign of perspiration. (As teenagers, they were used to that climate.)

After treating that man's injured feet, and giving him medicines, bandages, sterile water with which to wash his feet, and instructions on how to care for his feet, we also gave out about a dozen glasses to those in need . On our way back we reflected on our hiking trip..

We now understand why some sick people do not go to the clinic. How could a man, injured on the bottom of both feet like that, walk along those muddy trails? Could a mother with five feverish children, carry her six-month-old baby and a two-year-old toddler daughter and take the other three children that far? No way!

**

I remember sitting in the bow of the boat while we were cruising at night, and seeing ambient light being reflected in the river water.

I also remember many large size bugs. Once I saw a tarantula spider that was bigger than my spread-out hand. There were many other kinds of big bugs that I do not remember seeing before.

I remember many good sized bats flying around at night, in fact so many that I could hear their built-in radar beams reflecting off each other.

**

There are fresh water dolphin or porpoises in the Amazon River. They look pinkish on the bottom side instead of white such as in salt water porpoises. Therefore, they are called pink dolphin. Playfully, they jump out of the water, swimming along parallel to the boat, keeping up with the boat as they jump out of the water in a series of graceful jumps.

According to Amazon mythology and legend, at one time they were human, but for some unknown reason, they became pink dolphin. Nowadays, if a girl gets pregnant and no one knows who got her pregnant, she will claim she was swimming with the pink dolphin in the river and that the dolphin got her pregnant. This is strictly a folk story, an interesting but fictitious, impossible claim.

**

Sometimes we would see a six or seven-foot long snake, about two or three inches in diameter, with a big bulge a foot or two below its head. What had happened was that the snake caught and swallowed a small rat , cat, rabbit, chicken or some other such small animal, and was digesting it slowly. That snake probably wouldn't eat again for six to eight months or more, when that animal had been digested.

Snakes have a special jaw hinge that allows the bones to come apart so that its prey can pass through the jaw. The jaw then comes together and rehinges itself, and the snake is back to normal again.

**

For evangelist services along the Amazon, people will sit on hard benches or on the hard floor in temperatures of 90-95 degrees, for two or three hours without complaining and be happy to listen. Many of the women use a hand fan. Here in America, we sit on padded seats with backs, in air conditioned comfort and complain if the church service goes on much over an hour.

**

In my seven trips to the Amazon, some of us would jump off the boat and swim in the river to cool off after a long day's work. At the same time, some native boys at the other end of the dock, perhaps only 80-100 feet away, may be casting in throw lines with baited hooks and catching piranha. To the best of my knowledge, no one on an AMOR trip has ever been bitten by a fish of any kind.

**

Each day along the Amazon was very much the same for me, except for seeing different patients each day. In Brazil, just below the Equator, there are probably over 500 rivers that compose the Amazon River Valley, which gets 80-400 inches of rain each year. Severe flooding occurs often in this jungle rain forest. The temperature is 80-105 degrees Fahrenheit or higher year round. With water and hot temperatures, trees and plants grow fast year round.

**

Sometimes when two rivers meet or join, one of the rivers comes from the northern hilly area with blackish soil. The other river may come from a southern flat land area with brownish soil. When the two rivers meet or converge at an angle, the result is that one half of the new river on the north side is blackish, and the half of the river on the south side is brownish.

This is called the meeting of the waters, which results in a very obvious color line of demarcation going side by side for several miles downstream, until the colors progressively merge as the waters slowly mingle. If this merger takes place near a large city such as Santareem or Manaus in north central Brazil, it is such a tourist attraction that sightseeing boats come out to the center of the river to see and photograph this remarkable sight.

The large metropolis of Manaus is at the junction of the Rio Negro river from the north and the Rio Salimoes from the southwest. Their junction forms the Rio Amazon.

**

Often along the Amazon River, in a somewhat secluded pond or lagoon, there will be some 50-60 Victoria Amazona water lilies, which have enormous lily pads floating on top of the water. Some of these lily pads measure over six feet in diameter, with the outer edge turned up, forming a straight-sided rim of about three inches with a dish-like surface.

The greenish leaves seem to be quilted, due to thick veins radiating out from the center stalk on the underside of the leaf. These veins are filled with a gas which makes it quite buoyant. The lily is a night bloomer and has enormous flowers, ranging in size from eight to 10 inches in diameter. It blooms for two consecutive nights. The first night it has a whitish flower, the second night it turns to a pinkish or reddish blossom. The flowers have a crushed pineapple fragrance. This lily is considered to be the most spectacular of all lilies in the world.

Sometimes small animals or birds live on these large lily pads. Folklore legends report that a small baby could be supported safely on such a very large lily pad and take a nap on it. I would not advise that. But to prove a point, people have experimented and put a six pound weight in a shoe box lid and placed it at the center of a large lily pad. The lily held up that weight!

These large Victoria water lilies with their upright rim are most interesting and unusual.

They only grow in tropical or subtropical climates.

**

One day while walking along the riverfront, our group was waiting for our boat to leave. We saw a man making model boats and other items out of a thin, lightweight Balsam wood, which is often used to make model airplanes that fly. He had a half dozen different models on display.

Someone in our group asked him, "Can you make a model of our boat the size of that model?" first pointing to our boat and then to a certain model in front of us. He looked at our boat for a minute or two, and then answered, "Yes, I can do that." "We are leaving in a few minutes and won't be back for 10 days," we said. "Can you have it ready by 9:00 a.m. that day? We leave for the airport soon after we arrive back."

He took another long look at our boat and replied, "Yes, I can do that." "You're sure about that?" We asked again. "We leave soon after we get back." "Yes," he replied. "I'll have it ready by 9:00 a.m." Our final question was, "How much will it cost?" He quoted us an amount that was the equivalent of $20.00 in U.S. dollars. "OK," we responded. "It's a deal."

He was waiting for us when we returned 10 days later. The boat was ready also. It was well built and every bit as nice as hoped for.

That model boat is 42 inches long, 13 inches wide and 14 inches high and only weighs a few pounds. For many years, I have been giving several talks each year to church groups, school classes, civic clubs, and senior citizen groups, etc., about mission trips and travel experiences. I usually take the boat along. A picture or model is worth a thousand words.

**

River Boat on Amazon River

Chapter 7: Thailand and Chile

You never know when opportunity is going to knock!

Our church, which is a fairly large church, held a Mission Fair every fall. A half dozen missionaries, with whom we either have a special or family connection, or who are in the states on furlong, come and talk to us.

At this Mission Fair in the fall of 1996, I met Dr. and Mrs. John Gibson from Thailand. They would be returning to Bangkok in about five months. As we talked, Dr. Gibson told me that his hospital in Bangkok was taking its annual medical mission trip to northern Thailand in March of 1997. They had never had an optometrist on such a trip, and they needed one, so he invited me to come and go along.

After talking with my wife, I quickly agreed to go. Boy, was that a quick decision to go halfway around the world for a mission trip!

Dr. Gibson told me to bring the glasses to his parents' home near Orlando where they were staying, and he would ship them along with his family's luggage by boat to Thailand, and they would be there when I got there. That way I would not have to go through customs with them and would be saved all that hassle. "OK," I said. "I'll do that."

A few weeks later, I took the glasses to him. About two weeks before I was to leave for Thailand, I got an email from him, informing me that the glasses were shipped on the wrong boat and would not be there when I got there and asking if I could bring another set of glasses. "Yes," I emailed back. "I'll bring another set."

Then two days before I was supposed to leave, I got another email from Dr.Gibson. He was sick and would not be able to meet me at the airport. However, he had made all the necessary arrangements for me. If I would follow the following list of instructions, I would be okay. "That's fine," I emailed him. "I'll follow your instructions."

This was his list of instructions:

(1) When I arrived at the Bangkok airport on the specified time and date, I should go across the street from the main entrance of the airport to the airport hotel .

(2) Reservations for me had been made and paid for at that hotel. I should check in and leave all of the glasses at the front desk. Someone would pick them up later and drive them and other supplies up to the town of Nan.

(3) I should spend the night at that hotel. My tickets for the next days flight at 8:00 a.m. would be in the room which had been reserved for me.

(4) At 7:00 a.m., I should return to the airport and get on the 8:00 a.m. flight to Nan. When I got to Nan, an American man with a beard and wearing glasses would meet me. He would take care of me . He was the man in charge of the trip. (I wasn't told the man's name.)

(5) He, Dr. Gibson, would see me in Bangkok after the trip was over.

I thought to myself, "Boy, Dr. Gibson, this is really trusting in the Lord. Flying halfway around the world to meet some unnamed man with only his description to identify him. This is crazy." But I did it. (I also didn't tell my wife about this. She would have had a fit and never let me go.)

I arrived on schedule in Bangkok several days later. I had five suitcases of glasses plus one personal suitcase. Five of the six suitcases arrived promptly, and I loaded them on a cart and waited for the last one to arrive. As I waited, I watched the other passengers get their luggage and go through customs. The officials were opening every single bag, rummaging around inside and messing everything up. My heart sank. I could just imagine what was going to happen when they opened my suitcases and found over a thousand pair of glasses and me not being able to speak a word of their language to explain what I was doing with so many glasses. (That is part of the reason why I had tried to send the glasses ahead of time.)

Finally, my last bag arrived. It must have been the very last one on the plane, because they stopped running the conveyor belt. I was relieved that it had come, but I dreaded what would happen next. I loaded it on my cart with much trepidation in my heart and prayed for God's mercy and help as I approached the custom agent. All the rest of the agents had left, and he was the only one still there. I uttered another silent prayer and smiled at him as I handed him my passport. He looked at it, and then at me and the six suitcases. He smiled and waved me on without looking at any of them. He turned and headed for the door behind him. I uttered a prayer of thanks. That certainly was God's answer to my prayer, and I was certainly thankful.

I left the airport and pushed my cart full of suitcases before me to the hotel. I picked up my key, left the glasses at the front desk, and went to my room and found my ticket. So far, everything was going as planned. Since it was too late to eat out, I found a couple of Oats and Honey Granola bars, and that was my supper.

The next morning at 6:45 a.m., I checked out at the front desk and checked to see if the suitcases had been picked up. They had been, so I went across to the airport.

I walked from one end of the airport to the other but could not find the right airline. Finally, I checked with Northwest Airlines, the one on which I had arrived, and they told me I was in the international airport. The domestic airport for local flights was about a quarter mile out the door at the other end of the airport.

I rushed over there, following their instructions, and quickly found the right airline. I boarded a four-engine foreign made jet which I had never seen before. I quickly discovered that I was the only non-oriental on board the entire plane of about 60 passengers.

We made one stop on our way to Nan in the northern mountainous area of Thailand. Some passengers got off, and others got on board at that stop.

Finally, we arrived at Nan. When we got off, I looked around and did not see anyone who came close to matching the description of the man I was to meet. Unpleasant thoughts and fears started flitting through my mind as the minutes went by. Then, about 10 minutes later, I saw a bearded man come walking in. I was never so glad to see anyone as I was to see Steve Kavli, a total stranger. We greeted each other as he introduced himself. I guess that I stood out like a sore thumb, just as much as he did, in that crowd of Orientals. He took me to his home to meet his family and the rest of the mission team.

This mission team was mostly composed of Thailand preachers and seminary students, a Thailand medical school professor and several medical students, and a couple of American medical students doing a rotation in Thailand. Also there was a visiting doctor from the states and me, for a total of 28+. Steve, the bearded missionary from Nan, was the leader. His family came along also.

45

The next morning we started out in an seven car-and-van caravan, with one of the vans pulling a trailer on which was a good sized gas powered generator. As we crossed several mountain ridges, we zigzagged up and down the switch backs until we reached the town to which we were going. This mountain top town did not have a typical town square with trees and some statues. It had a soccer field instead. There were several stores on one side.

With the Thailand students, we divided into groups and visited every home in that town, plus all the surrounding areas.   All of the people were told to "come to the square when it gets dark." That sounded odd to me, until they explained that few if anyone in town had a watch.

Back at the square, several fellows used the soccer poles to hold up a large white sheet to be used as a screen stretched between them. (We had brought the screen with us.) Then the trailer with the generator was pulled into position, and we were ready.

As the sun disappeared in a blaze of color to the west behind the mountains, dusk approached and darkness came quickly.

Quietly the people came onto the soccer field, far more than we had imagined from the number of homes or buildings seen. Some of our students estimated there were 850-900 people present.

Finally, it was dark enough to start the program, and our leaders turned on the generator and then the switch to the movie projector, and the screen was illuminated with a bright light. Suddenly, a Charley Chaplin film started. You could hear a loud, "Ahhhhhhh" come from the audience, many of whom were seeing a movie for the first time in their lives. They were totally fascinated. Mesmerized might be a better word to use.

The sound track for the movie had been changed so that the spoken language was in Thai. Large roars of laughter came from the audience as Charley got into all sorts of trouble but somehow managed to avoid injury or death. If you have ever seen one of his movies, you know what I mean.

After this 10-minute film was over, and the audience was warmed up, and their curiosity had been aroused, then a film about the Good Samaritan was shown. It was filmed in Thailand with Thai actors speaking in Thai, dressed in Thai clothing and with the Good Samaritan riding on an elephant, which is typical of Thailand, instead of on a donkey.

The first priest who passed by the injured man in the ditch was dressed as a Buddhist priest wearing a Buddhist typical orange robe, and thus instantly identified as such by his orange robe. The second priest who passed him by was a Hindu, dressed in their typical garb, instantly known to the village people by his dress. Next, the Samaritan. came, saw the man, got down from his elephant, helped the man, pushed him up on his elephant, and took him to a nearby inn. You know the rest of the story. We could hear a hush fall over the audience as the film progressed.

At the end of the film, a Thailand preacher got up and delivered his message. The audience was responsive, and many came forward for counseling and to get a Bible in Thai.

The next morning, we had a medical clinic until about 2:00 p.m. before driving off to another mountain village and repeating the performance.

Later in the week, we stopped at a village where the previous year's team had been, so they showed the Thailand version of the Joseph-and-His-Coat-of-Many-Colors-in-Egypt story. This also drew a very good response from an enthusiastic audience.

Details about the trip: all week we slept in sleeping bags on foam rubber pads in school buildings, but one night we had to sleep in two-man tents because nothing else was available.

47

One can see why it is so important to have a local personal representative who plans every detail of one's trip and prepares properly for each aspect of the trip. All of the items we needed were waiting for us when we arrived and would be used the following year with another group.

We got used to "squatty potties" for bathrooms; cool to cold showers; eating strange or spicy foods; and bumpy, potholed roads. This was normal in many places, so we endured these "hardships" with smiles on our faces. That is how the other half of the world lives. Half of the world lives on beans and rice. Thailand has some very hot peppers, so hot that if you bite into one, you tasted it for a whole week.

Dr. Gibson and his wife met me in Bangkok when we returned. All in all, it was a very successful trip. Many, many people were witnessed to, and several thousand Thai Bibles and New Testaments were handed out. Many medical patients had been seen and were given medicines, and many visual problems had been solved with glasses and medications.

**

Shortly before arriving in Tokyo on my way back home, I looked out my window on the left side, and there was Mount Fuji glistening in all its majestic splendor. Its huge snowcapped balanced cone is one of the most perfect in the world. No wonder the Japanese are so proud of it. Praise the Lord for letting me see it on a clear day, and for giving me a left window seat so that I could have an unobstructed view of its 12,388 foot peak. What a wonderful, unexpected treat on the last day of my trip!

**

Several years later, the bearded missionary, Steve Kavli, and his wife stayed in our home while they attended our church's conference. Years later, their daughter attended Palm Beach Atlantic University here in town, and she visited in our home. We even held a party for her and her friends. She is a very nice and lovely girl.

**

On a mission trip to Santiago, Chile, I ran into my first road block--first ever. The customs officials declared that I could not take my glasses into the country because that would harm the local opticians and eye doctors. However, I could get my two suitcases of glasses back when I left. So I agreed. What else could I do?

However, the customs officials didn't say anything about the 60 pairs of reading glasses that I had in my personal luggage suitcase, so I entered the country with those 60 pairs.

I was the only medical person on the trip. All the rest were preachers and teachers. The next day I held an eye clinic in a church until all the glasses had been given out. Then I worked with the rest of the team as an evangelist. We spoke at different meetings. Then I helped distribute clothing and shoes to local orphanages.

All members of our team were hosted by different Chilean families. My host family consisted of a husband, his wife, and their 15-year-old son. The wife's mother lived in a small back apartment. The husband's parents lived a block away in their home. It was only a two-bedroom home, so I was given the son's room, and he spent the night with his grandparents but was back in time for breakfast. At night, he would stay until everyone was ready for bed, and then he would leave.

I only had one problem. I didn't speak any Spanish, and none of them spoke any English.
However, their son was a very bright boy. Several days earlier, he had gone to a computer store and bought a special English-Spanish program for his computer. On it, he would type in a question in Spanish, touch a button, and it would translate it and have it

printed in English for me to see. I would read the question, type in my answer, and touch a button, and it would print out the Spanish translation for him. We spent a lot of time going back and forth and laughing at some of the answers.

Every day I would go out with the team. Sometimes their son went along with me. One day I was scheduled to speak at a meeting in the seaport city of Valparaiso, some 50-60 miles away. I had to ride an inter-city bus to get there. Their son went along as my official helper, but I have a gut feeling that he was probably sent along so that I didn't get lost.. I was very thankful to have him along. We went over and back with no problems.

Their food was excellent and their hospitality was more than I could have expected. God's blessing from their Christian fellowship and love was much greater than I could ever have really expected. Our team went to serve the people of Chile, to share and show them the love of Jesus. Instead, we received from the Chilean Christians far more than we gave.

Caravan in Thailand

Chapter 8: Ukraine and Romania

John and Tommie Soileau, good friends of my wife and me, took an early retirement from Pratt Whitney and became Peace Corps volunteers. They were assigned to the Ukraine for two years, and thoroughly enjoyed their time there, making good friends with several families .there.

Several years later, John called me and asked if I wanted to go on a medical mission trip to Ukraine. After getting more information and talking it over with my wife, I agreed to go.

The trip was sponsored by Volunteers in Medical Mission (VIMM), a Christian medical organization which sponsors 15-18 such trips each year to various countries throughout the world.

We flew from the USA to London to Kiev, the capitol of the Ukraine, and then were bused about 100 miles westward to the city of Zhitomir, which became the hub of our operations.

Our team consisted of seven doctors, one optometrist, several nurses, and about 6-8 support personnel. We came from a number of different states, and several unusual backgrounds.

I knew only my two friends before the trip. Some of the others didn't know anyone else on the team before we departed from the states. However, we did have a common bond, and that was to share the love of Jesus with the Ukrainian people and with each other. Our team's purpose was to hold medical clinics; visit hospitals; and distribute shoes, socks, sweaters, and coats for the extremely cold winters; and school supplies to several orphanages. While talking to many of the children, they told us that before they entered the orphanage, they almost froze because they didn't have anything to wear in the cold, freezing winters and snow.

At each clinic an evangelistic message was presented, and each person who came to the clinic was given a Gideon Bible in the Ukrainian language if he could read. We received several thousand Gideon Bibles from a semi truck full of the Bibles at the Central Baptist church.

With Zhitomir as the hub of a wheel, each day we went out on a different spoke of the wheel to a town about 1-1 ½ hours away, where it had been arranged ahead of time and publicized for several weeks that the medical team would hold a clinic from 9:00 a.m. to 5:00 p.m. in that church on that date.

Literally thousands of dollars of medical supplies, eyeglasses, and clothing were furnished to the people who attended, plus the free medical care. Usually we had long lines of people waiting for us when we arrived . Usually, we could not quit at 5:00 p.m. as planned because we still had more people to see. Often, we were there until 6:00 p.m. or later.

All of our team members were hosted by different Ukrainian families. Usually two team members per family were housed, hosted and fed. My family consisted of the husband, Sasha; his wife; and their three teenage children. Sasha is a very popular man's name in the Ukraine. I stayed with two different families on my three trips there, and in both families, the husband was named Sasha and often a son is named Sasha.

In both cases, we were given the boys' room, and the children slept on blankets or rugs piled on the floor in the parent's room, or in a storage room. They are very generous.

Another thing we noticed about the Ukrainian people is that they have well trained singing voices. We heard their choirs, and they are wonderful.

Their food was excellent, and their hospitality was more than I could have expected. God's blessing upon our Christian fellowship was much more than I would ever have really anticipated. Our team went to help the Ukrainian people and to show and share with them the love of Jesus. Instead we received from the Christians of the Ukraine, far more than we gave.

**

Ukraine is considered to be the breadbasket of Europe. It is located in Europe, not Asia. At harvest time, one often sees harvested vegetables etc., lying in stacks or piles near the road waiting to be picked up. However, the lack of transportation is a problem.

**

In the Ukraine, away from the downtown areas, many small cities or towns have single dwelling homes which do not have much or any lawn or grass as we know it, that has to be cut weekly. The Ukrainians are very industrious and hard working and utilize every square foot of land that they own, to grow food. They are very practical.

Part of the land next to the house will be used for a garden, another section will have fruit trees, and another section will have fruit-bearing or berry bushes, etc. They can it or store it for winter.

One fellow I met worked a 40-hour-a-week shift in a factory and then came home and in the evenings and on Saturdays, made sausage in his garage and sold that in the market to make extra money.. That is using his head and his property, to their fullest capacity. Other people use their garage or basement for other kinds of side businesses.

Some people raise chickens for eggs and meat.. In the economy we have today, perhaps we should borrow these ideas from them and be this industrious ourselves.

**

When the Russians controlled the Ukraine, they built huge apartment buildings, with 100-200 apartments each. All the water, the heat, and the electricity to that apartment building was controlled by one central switch. If the government wanted to control that building, they could turn off everything and thus control those people easily.

**

ROMANIA

The year I was in Romania, we celebrated two Easters a week apart. The first Easter was the regular Easter, and the second Easter was the Eastern Orthodox Easter. The school children were particularly happy because they were given a holiday, and school was out for the whole week. (The two Easters are not always one week apart It varies. For instance, in 2008 the two Easters were five weeks apart. But again in 2009 they were one week apart

After landing in Budapest , Hungary, we drove by automobile across the border to Oradea, Romania, where we met our host, Pastor Elijah, at the seminary. Shortly after we arrived that afternoon, he guided us on a short city tour. At a certain intersection, he stopped the van we were riding in and pointed to a building in front of us. "See that building?" he asked. "Yes,'" we agreed. "Near the end of WWII, a Nazi inspector from Berlin was in town on a Sunday for an inspection. He noticed a large number of people going into the building. But the inside soon filled and many people overflowed and had to stand outside, listening to what was said through the open door."

"What are those people doing?" asked the inspector. "They are Christians going to church," replied the mayor. "Get a bulldozer tomorrow, and tear down that building," said the inspector. "That's an order. I will check back and see if it is down." "Yes sir," answered the mayor.

However, all in God's timing, the war ended that night, and his order was never carried out. God had worked a miracle.

We drove up the street a few blocks and saw the much larger church that the people had built several years after the war ended. The old building is now used for other church purposes.

Our leader Ken Winter preached on Sunday morning in church. On week days, I held eye clinics at several locations.

Our group traveled to several other towns in Romania. We stayed in their homes, ate with them and enjoyed their traditional dishes and their way of life.

When we returned to Oradea, we stayed in the guest rooms at the seminary. At supper time, the rest of our group was out elsewhere, so I went down to the student cafeteria where I had been instructed to go to eat. The students were off for the holiday, and there were only a few people there. I started talking to the man across the table from me

If my memory serves me correctly, his name was Thomas . He related this story to me:
Thomas was from London. He was an organ installer and repairman. Slightly over a year earlier, he had been in Romania to repair an

organ in a nearby town. On his way home, he stopped in to visit his friend, Pastor Elijah, at the seminary.

Most of the seminary buildings were completed, but the chapel building was only about 95% done. The seminary wanted an organ for the chapel because it would serve as a church for the people in that area of town. However, they didn't have the money, so they decided to complete the chapel building but leave an empty space where the organ would be placed later on. They were trusting that God would provide it, in His own time. After visiting a few days, Thomas returned to London.

News about organs travels fast through the organ repairmen and installers and organists. A few months later, Thomas heard that a big church in the London area had received a bequest from a wealthy woman, who was a member. She would give a new, bigger organ to the church if they would take out the old organ and replace it with her donation.

The next day, Thomas went to that church and asked to see the organ. Since they knew him from repair work that he had done before, they allowed him to inspect it. He measured it carefully and checked it out thoroughly. Next, he called pastor Elijah in Romania, gave him the details, and asked him if they were still interested. "Of course," Elijah answered. "It would really be a Godsend."

The church in the London area wanted the new organ, but they did not want to have someone take out the old one and leave the place in shambles, leaving them with an expensive repair bill. They couldn't afford that. However, if Thomas would remove the old organ carefully and do as little damage as possible to the woodwork, they would give him the present organ. He agreed. So he carefully took out the original organ to their satisfaction. He carefully used padded wrapping for all the pipes and disassembled all the rest of the organ, packing all the pieces carefully in boxes and marking them properly. Then he transported his newly-acquired organ to Romania by truck, which he had been working on it for over two months.

When I talked to him at supper that evening in the cafeteria, he stated that he was almost finished and invited me to come to the chapel the next day and see and hear it.

Do you remember Caesar's Roman adage? "I came, I saw, I conquered." This is my version: The next day, I came to the chapel, I saw the beautiful organ, and I was conquered by the beautiful music I heard him play.

God can work miracles if we only trust Him! The staff of that Romanian seminary had trusted that God would furnish them with a fine organ, and He did so.

Recently, I learned that a church here in the Palm Beach area had given their old organ to a church in Wisconsin under similar conditions. God is at work all the time.

**

About 25 years ago, in Romania there was a great need for local pastors. An unnamed wealthy churchman had agreed to give 50 scholarships, five each year for 10 years, to qualified Romanian students so they could go to a USA seminary and get their Master of Divinity degree. Pastor Elijah was one of those 50 students.

His theory in giving all those scholarships was that these new pastors would then return to Romania and minister to the Romanian people and fill a desperate need. However, only two of the 50 seminary students returned to Romania. All the rest stayed in the USA. Pastor Elijah married a girl from Florida that he met at school, but he took her to Romania. Many of the rest married here and stayed here.

An interesting point of information: Pastor Elijah's first name is Elijah. Their first child was a boy, and guess what his name is? Elisha. Just like in I Kings 19:16-19 and II Kings 2:1-13, we see that Elisha was the companion and successor to Elijah. In this modern day name case, someday this Elisha may possibly succeed his father Elijah.

A year or two after my visit to Romania, Elijah and his family were dinner guests at our home, along with other friends from our church. We had an enjoyable evening, reminiscing and talking about Romania and missions.

**

Note: While on mission trips to central and south America, I have asked the missionaries if they send their prospective seminary students to the USA. Practically all of them have emphatically told me, "No, because if we do, they never come back. They marry someone from the USA, get used to a different standard of living, and never come back, even though we need them desperately."

**

Chapter 9: Peru

After arriving in Lima, Peru, our medical group was split into two groups. One group flew on to Andahuaylas to the east in the mountains. The other group departed by bus for an orphanage about 20 miles from Lima in an arid, semi desert town.

I was in the mountain town group. The airport for this town was on a mountain top which had been leveled off to make the airport. The city was about 1500 feet lower in altitude.

Andahuaylas is an old town, and even in the summer at that altitude, is a very cold place.

Everyone wore a sweat shirt and a coat all the time. We were housed in an old fashioned hotel about two blocks from the orphanage, which was strictly for children under age 16. All the children were either orphans, or children abandoned by their parents and found on the streets, or their mother was on drugs or a drunk and had brought them in because she could not care for them.

First, all the children and the staff members were given checkups. Then we opened up the medical clinic for the rest of the townspeople. There was room for each doctor and each nurse, for the eye clinic, the pharmacy, and for the counseling and giving out Bibles and new

Testaments. Quite ideal. Long lines awaited us each morning. We saw people from 8:00 a.m. to 6:00 p.m. We were so busy, the need was so great. Some of them had walked for hours to get to the clinic.

We ate lunch with the children every day. A child was asked to bless the food at each meal, and some of those children had really learned how to pray. Of course, each one of us soon became attached to two or three of the children, and we talked and talked with them. My translator was a girl, age 13, who spoke English, Spanish, and Inca. She was one of my favorites.

On our last day there, we ate supper with the children. Then a big bonfire was built, and the children entertained us with folk dances complete with native costumes, native songs, and music. They were very good. The housemothers and staff had helped them make the costumes and practice the songs and dances. Each team member was presented with a small souvenir that the children had made. When we said goodbye the next morning, it was a tearful time. Lots of hugging. They hated to see us go, and they begged us to come back next year, which we promised to do. I went back four times.

When we flew back to Lima, we went to a very similar orphanage and worked in conjunction with our other group. We got to know these children, but I personally never got to know these children as well, probably because we were there only two days, whereas we had been five days with the mountain orphanage children. This group also put on a special program of singing and folk dancing in costumes for us. They hold a special place in our hearts.

**

One year, a few days before our departure from the USA, that mountain town area was hit by violence, revolt, strikes, and civil uprising, and two people were killed. Therefore, that part of the trip was canceled, and we stayed near the orphanage near Lima After working several days near that town, the mayor heard about us.

Since the next day was a national holiday, he invited our group to be spectators at an award ceremony he was giving to several local people for their achievements and then to watch the street parade from a specially raised viewing stand.

We met the mayor, the ceremony was very nice and dignified, and the parade was very colorful. There were many school groups, soldiers, bands, horsemen, singing groups, officials, etc. It lasted over an hour and a half. Quite interesting.

The following day, we were given the privilege of holding our clinics at the city hall in specially erected tents. Quite an honor, and we had a very good turnout of patients.

We held more clinics at several locations for the extremely poor people. Their living conditions were pathetic.

**

On another trip to the orphanage near Lima, Peru, one of our female team members was doing construction on a roof. When that part of the roof collapsed, she fell to the ground injuring herself. Our doctor took her to the best hospital in Lima, one of our nurses stayed with her overnight, and she flew back to the states a couple days later to be seen by doctors here. She recovered and went back to work.

**

After one of our trips to Peru, several in our group decided to take a post trip excursion and go to Machu Picchu, the legendary Lost City of the Incas. Totally hidden from below, it is high in the clouds.

In Cusco we marveled at the intricate masonry and startling building architecture of the Inca civilization that controlled most of South America over five and a half centuries ago.

Stones perfectly fitted together without mortar became impervious to earthquakes.

After a spectacular train ride through the stunning mountains from Cusco, we arrived at the town at the base of Machu Picchu. Then we got on a bus which had to zigzag its way up to the top to get to the entrance for the ruins.

Machu Picchu was abandoned by the Inca Indians many hundreds of years ago possibly because it was devastated by the plague or was overrun by a fierce jungle tribe. Row after row of its stone buildings and ruins stand in silent memory on the terraced ruins on the mountain top. Mysteriously, the stone walls of the ruins still stand today as if by magic, but almost all the roofs have rotted away or were blown away. As we walked, we were walking in the past!

When we relaxed a little, closed our eyes, and let our imagination roam, we could almost see the Inca Indians walking along those deserted streets in their bright costumes and working in the terraced fields. When we listened imaginatively, we could hear them laughing and talking together. Their happy echoes still remain!

Machu Picchu is a dream-like place with its beautiful scenery and unmatched beauty and with spectacular views of the snow capped Andes peaks in the distance.

**

Just as our bus was getting ready to go down, a native boy about 12 years old got on the bus. He made a bet with us that he could run down to the bottom quicker than our bus could follow all the zigzags in the road and get to the bottom. "If I do it," he said with a big grin," will each of you pay me 100 sol?" (That was about a quarter.)

We all agreed. Our bus started down the road, and he left the road and started down the rocky slopes to the next zigzag road below . He met us at that level. Our bus went on, and he went down the rocky slopes to the next switchback road and met us again.

We looked forward to seeing his smiling grinning face and waving hands each level down. Needless to say, he knew what he was doing and beat us to the bottom, where he collected his money. Our race with him made our trip more exciting. We were glad he won. Our driver said that he does that 6-8 times a day and always wins. Several other boys do that also. The bus drivers give them a free ride to the top.

** **

The above incident reminded me of another somewhat similar incident which happened in Cairo, Egypt several years ago. Our travel group took a Cairo bus tour . The bus stopped a half mile from the pyramids. Then we got on camels and rode over to the Sphinx and the pyramids At the pyramids, we got off and walked up to its base, where a guide explained many facts about how, why, and when the pyramids were built; who built them; and how tall they are. Then he asked us a question: "How many of you could climb all the way to the top and come back down in 20 minutes?" He pointed to the top with his outstretched hand. We eyed the pyramid and everyone shook their heads.

He said, "If each of you will pay me 20 piastres (worth about a quarter), I will do it in 12 minutes. I will take off my hat and wave to you when I reach the top. If I don't make it back in 12 minutes, you owe me nothing. Are you willing to bet me?" We all agreed.

He said, "We'll let the bus driver keep time, okay?" We agreed, but we also kept our own time.

He knew exactly where to go and possibly had smaller rocks placed strategically at certain places. He waved his hat at us from the top, and he was back down in ll minutes and 40 seconds.

We all paid up. He had made our trip more enjoyable and given us something unusual to talk about. We were smiling as we got back on our camels.

**

On one trip to Peru, while we were staying in a hotel near the orphanage close to Lima, we were there on a national holiday. The hotel consisted mostly of a series of one room apartments, which were filled with many families there all day to celebrate the holiday.

The extensive hotel grounds had a swimming pool, lots of swings, slides, teeter totters, etc., plus areas to play volleyball, basketball, and soccer.

Near the dining tables, a Peruvian pig roast had been set up. The cooks had been up before dawn, preparing the roasting pit, starting the fire and preparing and seasoning the pigs and wrapping them in palm or banana leaves. When the fire coals were just right, they lowered the two pigs into the pit, covered the pigs with more coals, and then with more palm or banana leaves, and then waited.

When the proper amount of hours had elapsed, they removed the two roasted pigs, each with a traditional apple in its mouth. For a fee, each guest was served a generous portion.

It was very interesting to watch and deliciously tasty to eat.

**

Each city has a street market area, consisting of several hundred booths, filled with all kinds of native vendors offering all kinds of products, foods, and goods for sale. Tourists can learn much about a country by browsing through the various booths and examining their products. Their native workers do very good, precise work, which is quite imaginative and skillful.

**

On another mission trip, the driver dropped off the medical team and supplies at the door of the church where we were going to have our clinics that day. Then he backed up the bus to park off to the side, so that the people could enter the church. Unfortunately, the left rear wheels slipped on the muddy grass and went into a ditch, and he could not get out. He had to call a tow truck to get it out.

**

A heavy rain the night before in Peru caused a lot of mud slides and covered the hairpin curves on the mountain road we were on to our destination at a mountaintop town. We got stuck on one sharp curve. We all got out to lighten the bus. It still could not move.

We tied a strong rope to the front of the bus. Some pulled while others pushed on the back, but with no success.

Finally, we collected as many tree branches and shrubbery branches as we could find, and put them under the rear wheels.. With half of us pulling, and others pushing, the bus finally inched its way forward until it was clear. Most of us were splattered with mud, but we all cheered as it finally escaped the mud. We drove on, happy to be moving

**

My most pleasant surprise: I was returning from a mission trip to Peru. Our group at the airport was having our tickets checked as we entered the waiting room before boarding our plane. The girl who was checking tickets to be sure that we were all supposed to be on that flight was a very pretty girl, wearing a name badge with the name "Rosemaria."

When I gave her my ticket, I said, "When I was younger, I dated a girl named Rosemaria, and she was a very pretty girl, just like you." She smiled and thanked me, and I entered the room.

About 10 minutes later, a loud speaker announcement stated that our plane would start boarding soon. All of a sudden, Rosemaria came up to me and said, "We have one open seat in first class. Would you like to have a free upgrade to first class?" Smiling, I said, "Of course! That's very nice of you. Thank you!"

I had made her day with a truthful compliment, and she returned the favor by making my day much more enjoyable with a better seat.

**

NICARAGUA

In Nicaragua, we had an extra long ex-school bus for transportation. The back of the bus stuck out about 10 feet behind the rear wheels. Many of the gravel roads do not have bridges over small creeks or dry creek beds that do not have any water except in rainy spells.

The road department just puts down a cement slab on the creek bed about two feet wide and the width of the road and that prevents the water from digging a deeper hole.

Often the road forms a "V" if the road bed slopes steeply down to the cement slab and then steeply up on the far side of the creek. We soon found out that our bus with its extra-long rear end could not maneuver over these deep dip creeks. As the front of our bus started up the far side on this deep "V" shaped dip, the rear end of the bus got hung up on the road behind it, and it got stuck.

Fortunately, we had a small two-seat truck along for short trips. We all got out of the bus and walked about a mile to our clinic site. The little truck carried our supplies and equipment, and we held our clinics.

While we were holding our clinics, the bus driver was finally able to back up the bus out of the creek bed. Then he backed it up about a half mile until he found a suitable spot to turn around. He cut the wires in the fence beside the road and dug up several fence posts.

Turning, he backed up into the field and then drove forward back onto the road facing the direction from which we had come.

Finally, he reset the fence posts, wired the fence back together, and he was finished At last, he backed up the bus and stopped just short of the creek where he got stuck. He waited for us to finish. His efforts were quite ingenious, I thought.

**

On one trip, our bus was going around a curve, and ahead of us we saw a motorcycle coming towards us on the other side of the road. The driver hit some loose gravel near the edge of the road and down he went and slid into the ditch. Fortunately, he was wearing a helmet. Our bus stopped, and our doctors got out and checked him over. Fortunately, there were no broken bones or serious injuries, just several bruises and an embarrassed ego. We picked his cycle up and put it on the road. It worked. There was no major damage, just a few scratches and dents. He started his motorcycle up, and with a wave of thanks, he drove off. We felt as if we had played the role of a good Samaritan.

**

On our second day, we were going into a different county or province than the day before. We stopped to get our certificate of permission to hold clinics, but we found out that we were denied permission because of some technicality. We sat and waited for several hours, while phone calls were made to the National Health Department in the capitol

Finally at about 5:00 p.m., the political problem was resolved, and we were given permission. However, we had wasted a whole day but were allowed to hold clinics the rest of the week. This shows the importance of having a very good in-country coordinator. Ours solved our problem.

**

One of our college girls wanted to be a dentist, so she was assigned to work with a dentist. After spending a day and a half carefully watching, the dentist showed her how to give the numbing shots before an extraction. She then gave the shots to a patient. Next, she was instructed on exactly how to extract a tooth. Soon, the dentist found the right tooth for her, and she extracted it under careful supervision. She was so proud of herself. She extracted several more that day. Someday, she may be a dentist.

**

On the way to a remote town in Nicaragua, we came down a long sloping road to a river. It was about 300 feet wide, with no bridge. We watched another car coming through the water towards us from the other side. When we saw that car could make it through the shallow river, we drove into the water and went across safely. Off to our right side on our way in were several three or four foot waterfalls. On our way in, we prayed for safety on our trip and asked that no heavy rain fall before we left because a heavy rain and the resulting rising water level could have prevented us from returning across that river that afternoon. Our prayers were answered. No heavy rain occurred.

**

A former president of Nicaragua owned several brick factories, so he built many roads using black bricks from his factories. On both sides of the roads, there is a four-inch wide cement rim band to hold the bricks in place. These roads are nice and smooth.

About 70 miles north of the capitol, Managua, there are many rice farms growing rice in flooded fields on both sides of the road. This continues on for many miles and is the center of their rice growing industry.

**

The Canyon of Somoto is near the town of Somoto, and about 20 miles south of the Honduras border. It is a very interesting place to visit. Upon arrival, we put on a life jacket and waded across the Coconut River, which is about 150 feet wide. Water comes up to the waist of a 6'1" man and much higher on 5'2" girls.

We held hands to avoid being swept away by the swift current or stumbling on the big river rocks on the bottom. Then we hiked about a mile along the river bank. Next, we waded back across the river again and hiked another half mile. Then we boarded several boats and went upstream a couple of miles. After that, we hiked another quarter mile and then jumped in and swam back to the boats.

This hike and swim combination is usually repeated because people enjoyed climbing part way up on the cliffs to a ledge 20-25 feet up and jumping in from there. Finally, we reentered the boats, and after going downstream about two miles, we got out. Then each of us got on a truck-sized inner tube and floated back to our first crossing point.

Dr. Spencer Meckstroth

A local young man swam along with each group of four or five inner tubes to speed us up and to guide our group through the rapids at various points. These canyons are not quite as steep or big as the U.S. Grand Canyon, but they were definitely well worth our time.

**

Chapter 10: Ecuador

Leaving our base camp in Ecuador, on our first day trip to serve a mountain top village in the high Andes, our bus rounded a curve in the road ahead, and we saw one of the tallest and most beautiful snow-capped mountains few people from the USA have ever seen. Its name was Cotopaxi, quite pronounceable in English. It is an active volcano: 5897 meters, or 19,800 feet high.

Our bus stopped so that our medical team could disembark and take a short trek over rough lava for a short distance to a lookout point. Our group walked in single file, avoiding huge rocks and deep gullies on the rocky cinder path.

Suddenly, we stopped in awe as the full mountain came into view before us, glistening in all its royal majesty.

Before long, the sun slid behind a dense cloud . The cool breeze suddenly turned into a bitter wind, and we were pelted with a blast of swirling snow for several minutes. We were not prepared for this and shivered in our coats.

Soon the sun reappeared, flirting with the clouds and warming up our group. We enjoyed a comfortable stroll back as we skirted the pockets of snow over the rocky lava path. Some of the pockets of snow were protected from the warmth of the sun by huge overhanging rocks. Technically, they could be called miniature mountain glaciers if they didn't melt completely each year.

**

On another day on our way to a town in the high Andes, the bus carrying our medical team passed on the outskirts of a tiny village alongside the road. Among the 14-15 houses and sheds, we could see a small church beside a school building, with 15-20 students playing outside on their dilapidated swing set.

Since one of our interpreters knew the pastor of that church, who also was the school teacher, we stopped to say hello. He was delighted to see us and our interpreter. The week before, he had told her that he wanted to start teaching his students to memorize verses from the Bible.

However, all he had was a tiny pamphlet-like book of John and another gospel tract providing the Plan of Salvation and four verses from Romans (3:23, 5:8, 6:23, and 10:9). He worried that he would have to write out the verses for each child. For several days he had been praying about how to do this.

He was overjoyed when we gave each child a New Testament in Spanish, and a couple extras, and gave him a Bible. "Praise the Lord!" He exclaimed. "This is God's answer to my prayers."

**

Once I was flying out of Miami to meet a group of doctors who were flying out of Atlanta. We were to meet in Quito, Ecuador. My plans were simple. My plane arrived an hour before theirs, so I would get my luggage and go through customs and then wait for their plane to come in and meet them just outside of customs. They had my hotel reservations and had made our transportation arrangements.

I easily cleared customs with my luggage, and everything was fine. I went over and waited for their plane to arrive. Soon their plane arrived, but none of their group arrived.

I checked with the information desk and found out what had happened. I learned they would arrive the next morning at 9:00 a.m. The way I understood it, they had missed the plane in Atlanta, due to bad traffic conditions and a flat tire.

There was a contact man I was supposed to meet, but I only knew his name as Thomas, and. I couldn't find him. Therefore, I was in a pickle. They had my hotel reservations, and I didn't even know the name of the hotel in which I was supposed to stay.

Our contact man couldn't find me either, so he called the rest of the group in Atlanta and told them I was missing. They called my wife and told her I was missing. She called our pastor, who called our deacon prayer chain, and soon everyone was praying for me. This happened to be the day that my first grandson, Jordan, and my first granddaughter, Megan, were graduating from high school. It was also the day that my son-in-law, Greg's, grandmother died, so it was a day fraught with emotion for my family back home.

Back in Quito, I uttered a silent prayer and headed for the information desk.

Fortunately, there was a bilingual clerk on duty. I asked her for the name of a nearby hotel that was safe. I didn't want to get mugged or robbed. She gave me a business card for a hotel and said, "This hotel will be safe and is nearby."

I got a taxi, and I gave the driver the card. He took me to the hotel, where I spent the night. The next morning I was back at the airport by 9:00 a.m.

While waiting at the customs exit with all my suitcases beside me, a man came up to me and asked, "Are you Spencer Meckstroth?" "Yes," I answered. "You must be Thomas, our contact man." He nodded his head, "Yes."

He phoned my wife on his cell phone, and I assured her that I was safe and sound and all right.. She told me about all the phone calls and the prayer chain. I was amazed and also rather embarrassed at all the commotion I had caused when Thomas and I couldn't find each other.

Thomas then called the group in Atlanta and told them I was safe and waiting for them. Together, we waited for their group's arrival. We were glad to see each other.

What a mess that was, all caused by a missed flight. Fortunately, everything turned out fine. It just proves that we have to be flexible and careful.

**

Near closing time on one of our medical mission trips to a town in the High Andes of Ecuador, a 45-year-old man came riding up on a donkey to our medical clinic, escorted by another man. He was soaked with blood in the groin area.

Following is his story: Several years before, he had been up on an eight or nine foot high roof , which he had been repairing. Somehow, he had slipped and fallen on his stomach, face down. He had landed in his groin area on top of a jagged metal fence post. With all his weight pressing down on that area of his body, extensive damage was done to his male organs by the fence post.

Fortunately, some other people saw this happen and immediately stopped the bleeding. Soon, he was taken by car to the emergency room of a major hospital in the nearest big city. They did the best they could with their repair surgery. His injuries had healed satisfactorily, and he had gotten along fairly well for several years.

The night before he came to our clinic, he and his brother-in-law had gone to a bar for a drink. After a while, his brother-in-law got in an argument with another fellow, and soon they were fighting. Then this other fellow's buddy joined in, and they were both beating up on the brother-in-law.

This man had tried to help his brother-in-law, but one of those fellows kicked him several times in the groin area, and he fell down. At his terrified screaming, the two assailants fled.

Other people in the bar stopped the new bleeding and carried him to his home nearby. No cars were available to take him to the hospital.

The next afternoon, some friends told him about our clinic, so his brother-in-law lifted him up on his donkey and brought him to our clinic.

When our doctors saw him and his blood-soaked clothes, they took him to our improvised exam table and removed the bloody mess and cleaned him up.

Appalled at all the damage that had been done, the doctors realized that his case was beyond their skills, considering the equipment and facilities available. Also considering that it was quitting time, and that we could not give him the proper follow-up care he would need (we were going back to the USA the next day), our doctors thought it in the patient's best interest that we drive him to the hospital where he had been treated before.

Therefore, we drove him to that hospital, and they took care of him. I never did hear what happened to him. I have often wondered.

**

On one medical mission trip to a town in the High Andes of Ecuador, the only road to that town was a gravel road that ran across the ridge crests of mountains. On both sides of the road the mountains sloped down rapidly. Most of the time, the road was only wide enough for one car or truck. We had spent the whole day working at that town, and we were returning back to our base camp.

Half way out to the main road that we would eventually meet, several of the girls in our group told our leader, "We have to go to the bathroom right now! It's urgent! We can't wait another 20-30 minutes!"

When he was appraised of the situation, our driver looked forward and saw no cars coming. Then he looked in the rear view mirror and saw no cars coming. Therefore, he stopped the bus.

All the men were instructed to get off and go down on the left side. All the women were instructed to get out and go down on the right side. Everyone did as instructed. By doing this, no one could see over the top to the other side, and everyone had a certain amount of privacy, enough to satisfy the modesty of most people.

Soon everyone came back to the bus, relieved and smiling again. It worked, but what a way to go to the bathroom on a cold, breezy day. We all had a good chuckle about it.

**

We were traveling on a lonely road in the High Andes. The mountain homes were few and far apart. Many of the homes had thatched roofs and had a stone fence around a small family compound. Several pigs, sheep, chickens, and goats wandered around. Two or three llamas were usually tethered to a stake so that they could eat the surrounding grass.

We don't know if the llamas are kept by the mountain folk so that they can be used as pack animals or if they are kept so that their wool can be sheared off each spring and used to make clothing. Once we saw a herd of 25-30 wild llamas clustered together about 40-50 feet from the road. Of course, we stopped for pictures. Wild llamas can be vicious if a person gets near their young ones. Also, llama spit is extremely caustic and can ruin a pair of shoes quickly. Because we knew this, none of our group got close enough for that to happen.

**

Arriving at a certain mountain town, we quickly unpacked and started our clinics. While we were eating our lunch at noon, our translators named and pointed out seven volcanoes. Imagine that! From our vantage point, we could see seven sizeable volcanoes, all to the east of the town in which we were.

**

One time in the High Andes, our base camp was at a church camp built at a much lower altitude. It was only four to six miles, as the crow flies, from a volcano that had a continuous spiral of smoke coming out of it each day. It had a minor eruption over 20 years earlier. Each day, we would check the volcano for any unusual activity, before we zigzagged up the mountain roads to the mountain top towns where we held clinics.

**

On May 27, 2010, Mount Tungurahua erupted in Ecuador, causing evacuations of hundreds of people from villages nearby, as molten volcanic lava flowed down the slopes. Fumes and ash smoke clouds billowed several miles above its 16, 479 foot crater. It is just south of Banos and east of Ambato. Possibly, it was the mountain near our camp. We're not sure.

**

On one trip, our team had just completed a weeklong visit to a small remote town high in the mountains of South America. We had given Spanish Bibles to all who could read.

Our group consisted of a medical mission team, and a daily Bible school team. Our preaching team held an evangelistic meeting each night, and during the daytime visited people throughout the area. By prearrangement, the school was closed for the days we were there, so that we could use it for our clinics. Each day, we were deluged with hundreds of patients, who waited patiently for hours in long lines.

Shortly before closing time on our last clinic day, a lady who had been to our clinics several days earlier, came up to me with her Bible in her hand and her finger inside, marking a certain page to which she wanted to refer.

First of all, she said, "I want to thank your group for giving me this Bible--and glasses so that I can read it. It is the first book I have ever owned. Someone told me to start reading with the Book of Matthew and I did so. Now I have finished the first 10 chapters. I read about Jesus going from town to town, preaching the gospel, healing the sick and injured. He healed people with all kind of diseases. He helped the blind to see again. He healed children in several towns. He helped the people, and He fed many people."

"As far as I am concerned, the day your group came to our town, is the day Jesus came to our town. Your doctors have given us medicine to heal sickness and diseases, you have treated our children, some of whom were close to death. You have given us glasses so that we can see and read again. Your dentists have removed bad, infected teeth from many people, and now their pain has been relieved. Your nurses have taught us how to use boiling water and properly clean and bandage injures so they don't get infected. Your group brought us food and helped us in many ways."

"Your daily Bible school teaches our children about Jesus and teaches them songs about Him. Each day as I go to work, I hear the children singing--as loudly as they can--these joyful songs about Jesus and His love."

"Every evening your preachers preach the gospel and teach us more about Jesus. In the daytime, they visit the sick and lonely in our town and even visited people in jail.

Tomorrow your group will baptize us before you leave."

"But best of all, last night after listening to the preacher, I went forward and accepted Jesus as my Lord and Savior. Hallelujah, praise the Lord. You gave me a Spanish Bible, and now I can read it every day. Thank you again and again. We hope your group comes back to our town next year. You have brought Jesus with you to our town."

What a compliment at the end of our trip!

**

On one of our High Andes trips, one of our team members got quite sick. Our doctors think it was because she had not been drinking enough water and at those high altitudes, that caused her problems. Our doctors put her on an I.V. overnight, and by the next day she was okay again. She learned her lesson the hard way.

**

The equator crosses Ecuador about 10 miles north of downtown Quito. The exact position of the equator is marked by a black line or stripe on the ground through the park that surrounds the monument.

Many others and I have had their picture taken straddling the equator, with one foot on the north side in the northern Hemisphere, and the other foot on the south side in the Southern Hemisphere. That seems to be the most popular pose. I have been there twice.

**

Also, there is a rather unique chapel built exactly on the equator. Half of the chapel is in the northern hemisphere, and the other half is in the southern hemisphere. Services are held there every Sunday and on special occasions. The equator runs east and west right down the center of the main aisle of the church. The pulpit also sits on the equator. If the priest or preacher is directly behind the pulpit, he is standing with one foot in the northern hemisphere and the other foot in the southern hemisphere. He truly is speaking to a world wide audience, to the four corners of the world. Half of the seats are in the northern hemisphere and half are in the southern hemisphere.

**

Another 150 feet west of the chapel is a 100 foot high stone tower, about 40 feet in diameter, with a very large metal globe on top. It is also a museum. People can ride an elevator to the top, survey the surrounding area from that elevated vantage point, and then slowly walk down the curving, gradually sloping incline walkway, and look at the various exhibits about Ecuador on their way down. This is a very interesting method of learning about Ecuador.

This equatorial line was set by a Frenchman in 1736. However, modern GPS measurements have determined that this line is about 150 meters off. Nonetheless, that doesn't seem to matter to the thousands of tourists who visit this spot each year.

**

Ecuador is home to a certain kind of palm tree that grows very large clusters of nuts about two inches in diameter. These nuts have a brown skin and a white center. As they mature, the white center turns hard to an ivory-like substance and can be carved into various shapes and figurines or souvenirs. Outside of animals, it is the only source of replaceable ivory in the world. The souvenir shops at the Equator park have many of these ivory items.

**

Downtown Quito has a very large cathedral. The sanctuary is very beautiful. There is a museum on several lower levels below the main sanctuary. Many mind-boggling exhibits go back to the days when the Europeans discovered Ecuador. For those who are interested in history, this is a must-see place to visit.

**

Leaving Ambato on one of our day trips for a medical clinic in a mountain town, we traveled on a serpentine dirt road towards the tallest mountain in Ecuador. Mount Chimborazo is 6,310 meters(21,190ft) high. Snow capped year round, it is beautiful to behold. Using binoculars, we watched two groups of mountain climbers working their way up towards the peak.

**

GPS systems are a big help in finding one's way to a specific address in our country, and in many foreign countries they will probably work fine also. GPS systems notify their users in advance that they are soon approaching a turning point. If a turning point is missed, the GPS will tell its user to turn around and recalculate his position. It will even tell its user when and where to turn again.

However, in some of the more remote areas of our world, streets and roads are no more than a dirt road which is unmarked and possibly unnamed. Homes and buildings often do not have numbers, etc.

I doubt if it is possible to use a GPS system there, but they certainly are useful where streets are named and numbered. Otherwise, it is always best to hire a local driver who knows his way around the area and countryside.

**

Chapter 11: Ethiopia, Kenya, and African Safari

In Ethiopia there are numerous refugee camps with thousands of refugees living in them.

Over 200,000 people were displaced when violence flared between government forces and rebel fighters, so they fled the conflict to stay alive. These are people (farmers, workers, etc.) from small farms and villages in a country next to Ethiopia.. .

In other places, suddenly a sizable group of greedy gun-toting bandits had appeared and at gunpoint forced the local people to flee for their lives or be shot. After some were killed in cold blood, the rest fled. The bandits followed them to the border of Ethiopia and forced them to cross into Ethiopia. Then leaving a few armed bandits near the border to prevent the people from returning to their homes, most of the bandits returned to the abandoned towns and homes and villages which they claimed for their own by taking possession of the now-empty homes and then continued living there and cultivating their stolen farms and running the small businesses.

Back in Ethiopia, the refugees had no means of support, or any place to live. They were completely destitute. So the Ethiopian government built a large number of small homes about 15 x 20 feet for each family. They built cement block homes with corrugated sheet metal roofs. There was a hand-pumped water pump in the center of the compound, and nearby there was also a pair of public toilets for men and women. We walked through one of these refugee camps, and the filth was unbelievable.

**

Driving or walking through a good-sized city in Ethiopia, one sees shepherds herding a flock of sheep, goats, or cows. The animals have the right-of-way, and cars or trucks stop and let them pass by. While driving through the dusty, dry countryside outside of the cities, one sees nomad shepherds with a flock of sheep/goats moving along slowly while the animals are grazing. The shepherds are dressed like Moses in the movie, "The Ten Commandments." Looking closely at the ground around them, in that desert-like area, there doesn't seem to be much grass or many bushes for the sheep to feed on, but apparently there is some. I guess it's not much different from Biblical days. Remove the automobiles and electricity, and it would probably be almost identical, I dare say.

In Ethiopia there are many people with leprosy, which is a big problem. We see them in our clinics, with parts of their fingers or toes gone, eaten up by the disease. Sometimes parts of their nose or ears are missing, or they have big sores on their faces.

We wear plastic gloves when working in areas of high incidence and wash frequently with alcohol.

We walked thru a leprosy colony one day and found it depressingly filthy, but not nearly as bad as the refugee camps. Years ago, there was no cure for leprosy. Today, modern medications will stop it but will not replace areas or parts eaten away.

Helping lepers with their vision is usually the same story. We find out what they need as far as glasses are concerned and fit them so

84

Better lighting would helpBetter lighting would help
even more. For some reason, they seldom think about moving the
light closer to what they wish to read or sew. Bigger bulbs help
noticeably. Occasionally, one or both ears have been eaten away, and
holding the glasses in place is a problem.

In Ethiopia checking lepers who have a reading problem, we have lines
of Arabic words in different sizes to check how well they can see.

However, if a woman is a seamstress and sews all day, she is more
interested in seeing to sew than she is in reading. Perhaps she is
illiterate and can't read, so reading means little to her. However,
being able to thread her needle and sew a straight line or a certain
design neatly and properly is what interests her. She has her own
priorities and has brought her needle and thread to check if her
eyesight is good enough so that she can work again.
.
When she has threaded her needle and taken several stitches
successfully, and we see she is smiling in approval, we know she is
happy with her new glasses. Now she can earn a living again. We
stress to her the importance of good lighting for the best results.

**

Leper men who make pottery, which they paint with intricate designs
to sell in the markets, will do the same. They will bring in some
small pottery items, to check out the new glasses we give them, to
be sure they can see the designs sharply enough to continue working.
They always start smiling when they are satisfied that they see well
enough. Now they can earn a living again. We stress the importance
of lighting to them also.

**

There are numerous pizza restaurants in Addis Abba ,Ethiopia.
One member of our medical mission team bragged to the rest of

85

us that he could eat the spiciest pizza ever made. He had never run into any pizza that was too hot for him to eat.

To prove his point, he showed us a small vial of hot sauce. "I made this myself," he bragged, "so that I can add it on and make any pizza more to my taste. It is made from several different kinds of very hot peppers and made from my secret formula."

One day our native driver heard him brag and told our leader that there was one pizza restaurant in town that featured a "fire" pizza that was extremely hot.

That night, our leader, John McNally, asked our group if we wanted to eat pizza that night at a very good pizza place that featured several kinds of pizza unknown to us.

"Yes," we said. "Let's go."

At the restaurant, Our waitress pointed out that one of the items on the menu was for "fire" pizza. "It makes your mouth burn," she said. "It's too hot for most people," she continued.

One man challenged the braggart in our group. "If you order that fire pizza and can eat all of it, I'll pay for your pizza and mine. But if you can't eat your pizza, then you have to pay for yours and mine. Okay?" "Okay," responded the braggart. "You're on."

The rest of us ordered ordinary pizzas.

Soon the pizzas arrived, and we all watched. The braggart grinned, opened his mouth, took a big bite of fire pizza, and started to chew on it. Quickly, tears came to his eyes. He started sweating, gagging, and turning red. Finally, he had to take a drink of ice cold coke to cool off his mouth. He admitted he had met his match. He paid off his bet.

Most Ethiopian foods are more spicy than a lot of Americans' taste buds prefer.

**

Before going on a medical mission team to Ethiopia, we had cautioned all the members of our team not to have anything in their carry-on luggage that could possibly be construed to be a weapon of any kind.

After arriving there, we had a busy week of clinics. On the final day, we closed the clinic at 6:00 p.m. and took our group to a local marketplace for some shopping. Of course, there were a lot of unusual items that we never see here in the states. We split up into groups of three persons for safety reasons, as different threesomes went up and down different aisles, and we met two hours later . When everyone had done all the shopping they desired, we went to a restaurant, then to our hotel, and we packed to go home the next morning.

The next morning we checked in all of our luggage except for the small carry-on bag allowed each passenger. Finally, we went to the waiting area for our flight number.

We were sitting there, patiently waiting, when one of the customs officials came up to our group and called out our leader's name. They asked him to go with them.

They opened up a suitcase with his name on it and showed him the two dueling swords inside. They had been detected by the X-ray scanning device.

"But that is not my suitcase," he said.
"Then how did your name get on it?" they asked.

He shook his head in bewilderment. Then, looking on the other side of the name tag, he found the name of one of the ladies in our group who had bought the swords and put them in a bag at the market. No one in our group saw her buy them, and she had packed them in her check-in suitcase, thinking that since they had been checked in, it would be no problem.

All of our suitcases, filled with clinic supplies on our way to Ethiopia, had our leader's name on them. By accident, somehow she had put his name tag on her suitcase. Since they were checked in, and she didn't have access to them until we got off the plane, she may have kept them. I'm not sure.

**

In both Ethiopia and Kenya, water is very scarce. On the streets there are many water salesmen in trucks, wagons, and carts, selling water. People will bring a container to them and they will fill it up out of a spigot and charge them so much, and away the people go.

Water should never be bought on the street. Even if it is bottled water as we have here, someone may have found an empty bottle and filled it up with regular water and put the cap back on it. If water is bought, the seal should always be checked to make sure the seal has not been broken. The people of Ethiopia may be worlds apart from our people in regard to language, clothing apparel, and culture-wise, but many people in each country are on the same page in regard to having a desire to know Jesus and to live a Christian life.

**

Kenya sits squarely on the equator, dividing the country into two halves. Higher elevations are quite cool. Lower altitudes can be very hot. Mount Kenya at 17,058 feet is Africa's second highest peak and is a popular hiking destination. We held a week of medical clinics at several churches in Nairobi, where AIDS and HIV are big problems.

Since Sam, one of the members of our medical mission team to Kenya, was a native of Kenya, he pre-arranged--after the medical mission trip was completed--for those of our group who wished to take a brief safari (the Swahili name for journey) to do so.

We went to the Serengeti Game Preserve and spent a night in tents at the Keekorok Lodge. We traveled in Land Cruisers past massive baobob trees, the sequoias of Africa. They store water in their hollow trunks, and their upper branches grow twisted all around as if they are frantically seeking water. They are called upside down trees by the natives.

Elephants rub their sides against the large Baobob trees, leaving telltale scars of missing bark. A herd of elephants crossed the road ahead of us, oblivious to the fact that we are there. They towered above our Land Cruisers. Protected by their crinkled gray skin, their long, skillful trunks can be used to grasp food and feed themselves. On one side of the road was a herd of elephants, while on the opposite side were some crocodiles, who were sunning themselves on a riverbank. A bunch of Wart hogs snorted their way past us.

Looking up in the trees, we noticed a pair of spotted cheetahs and a variety of birds.

Wildebeests by the thousands and zebras by the hundreds were grazing peacefully together. All humans have different fingerprints, and all zebras have different striping.. Wildebeests look like a strange combination of several animals: The shaggy head of a buffalo, the horns of an antelope, and the strange-looking legs of an awkward horse.

Another herd of giraffes came into view, in which were a couple of newborn giraffes standing on their long, wobbly legs and dangling a pink umbilical cord. On the other side of the road, a herd of zebras was seen, with several females giving birth to babies as we passed by.

We noticed several packs of hyenas roaming around, looking for a carcass or animal to devour. Our driver was always on the lookout for more animals.

Finally, we saw a pride of lions: a large male with a shaggy thick mane taking a nap on a small hilltop, with five lionesses sleeping and several cubs playing nearby. Lions often sleep 18-20 hours a day and hunt at night. No one bothers them. They are the King of beasts.

The sleeping facilities at the Keekorok Lodge were surrounded by a seven-foot fence topped with barbed wire. It probably would not stop a lion if he really wanted to come in, but it was the best that could be done. A sputtering generator electrified the fence all night long.

Alert armed guards patrolled the grounds at night. Several carefree baby gazelle ran around playfully and chased each other in a game of tag. They were safe if they stayed inside the fence near the lodge office. To the west are fine views of the African bush and majestic sunsets.

Elaborate candlesticks illumined the room that evening as dinner was served in the lodge's dining room with lovely china and fine silverware. Afterwards, in the dark, we made our way back to our tents, following the paths with our flashlights. We all slept in nice two-man tents on comfortable beds--definitely not a rugged campout.

We heard lions roar off and on all night, some of them quite nearby. Some of us had a hard time going to sleep. We prayed often for God's protection and safety. Up at the crack of dawn, our guide discovered a fresh zebra carcass slightly over a hundred feet from the compound in which we were staying. Several vultures were working on it already. All things considered, it was a good safari.

**

Chapter 12: Camels, Puppetry, and Costa Rica

Camels

The word Camel or camels is mentioned 42 times in the Bible--more times than many other words. Camels were used for traveling, especially across deserts, both for cargo or for riding, and sometimes for war. They were frequently called "ships of the desert" for two reasons: (1) they move both left legs and then both right legs, giving them a rolling motion like ships on the seas, and (2) they carry cargo across the desert like ships carry cargo across the seas. The desert would be uninhabitable without the camel and the palm tree. Their milk is a luxury much esteemed by many. During Biblical times, and up until the 1920's-1930's, they were the only way to travel across long, sandy desert areas. Then cars and trucks started to replace them.

In the Bible, a man's worth was described by the animals he had, not the amount of gold and silver he owned. (See Job 1:3 and Job 42:12.) Solomon is an exception. Camels were highly regarded, valuable, and numerous. See below.

Judges 6:5	Camels without numbers
1 Kings 10:2	The Queen of Sheba came with a great train and camels with presents for Solomon
2 Kings 8:9	A king sent a 40-camel caravan with presents for Elisha
1 Chronicles 5:21	50,000 camels were taken away
2 Chronicles 14:15	Sheep and camels were taken away in abundance
Ezra 2:67	435 camels were owned
Job 1:3	Job had 3,000 camels before his trials, plus a list of other animals
Job 42-12	Job had 6,000 camels after his trials, plus a list of twice as many other animals

There are two species of camels.

Bactrian camels are the two-humped camels that live mostly in southwest Mongolia and northwest China in mountainous areas. They have thick, hairy wool coats and are better suited to cold, freezing climates. They shed their heavy coats in summertime. Most are domesticated for work. There are probably less than 2,500 Bactrians left in the world.

The one-humped Arabian camels are the other species. They have longer legs and slimmer bodies and live mostly in warmer regions. Most are domesticated and carry packages and people across deserts. Camels have tough padded feet that can walk over burning sand without a problem. They have long, bushy eyelids to protect their eyes from blowing sand, and they have bushy covers for their nostrils also. Arabian camels are a trifle shorter and less heavy than the 1,400 pound Bactrian species. There are several million Arabian camels in the world. Camels are used for transportation, to make clothing from their wool, for their milk, and for their meat. Camel racing is popular in some countries.

Some of the faster Arabians have been bred for swiftness, and their speed is almost unbelievable: 900 miles in eight days, quite a record. Some camels can run as fast as 40 miles per hour.

Both species have thick, hairy lips; a tough tongue; and sharp teeth. They can easily eat prickly bushes with thorns, spines, barbs, and bristles common to desert plants. Their upper lip is split, and the two sides move separately so that they can grasp food. Camels concentrate their fat in humps instead of spreading it out. Otherwise, they would be wrapped in a sheet of fat, which would hold in too much heat. They absorb energy from their fatty hump if they do not eat. A camel can go several days without drinking any water. Afterwards, a grown camel can drink up to 30 gallons of water in 10 minutes but needs lots of salt to absorb it. God's wise creation!

A newborn calf or baby weighs about 80 pounds and has long, gangly legs. It is about four feet high at the shoulder. About two hours after birth, it can walk

**

In Genesis 37:23-28 we read that after Joseph's brothers had stripped him of his colorful coat, they cast him into an empty pit. "And they sat down to eat bread: they lifted up their eyes and looked, and behold a company of Ishmaelites came from Gilead with their camels bearing spicery and balm and myrrh, going to carry it down to Egypt." So Joseph was sold and went to Egypt where he was sold again.

Since camels were the only animals able to carry heavy loads across the deserts, these verses verify that merchants had organized camel caravans to and from Egypt by that time in history.

**

Since the three wise men from the east who visited Jesus at his birth in Bethlehem are mentioned together several times in Matthew 2:1-12 , they must have traveled together from the east. Probably for safety and protection purposes of their rich gifts, they traveled in a camel caravan across the deserts. They followed the same star.

In Matthew 2:12-23 we read that God warned Joseph in a dream to take Mary and the baby Jesus from Bethlehem to Egypt to escape the wrath of King Herod. (That was a distance of 200-250 miles, depending on where they settled in Egypt.) Later, Joseph learned in a dream that King Herod was dead, so they returned to Nazareth. Probably both trips were made by camel caravan so that they would be safe and have protection from bandits etc. on those lonely desert trails.

**

Riding a camel looks something like riding an electronic bull in a bar or at a circus.
God must have a good sense of humor. It's hard for a person not to grin when he looks at the animal.

Jesus used a camel to point out our critical hypocrisy when we seek perfection in unimportant, mundane parts of other people's lives, yet ignore or totally neglect rightness in important aspects of our own life, such as justice and mercy and faithfulness. ("Ye blind guides, who strain out a gnat and swallow a camel." Matthew 23:23-24) We need to inspect our lives and see if we pass that test. If we don't, we need to admit our flaws, reflect on them, and correct them. In Luke 18:25, Jesus said, "It is harder for a camel to go thorough the eye of a needle than for a rich man to enter the Kingdom of God."

**

One day in Ethiopia, as our medical mission team was returning from a long day at the clinic, our bus drove past a zoo which had a roadside sign announcing that they offered camel rides for a certain price. The price seemed reasonable, and several of our members wished to take a camel ride, so our driver turned the bus around and went back to the zoo

The camel was squatted down on all four legs beside a three-foot high platform. One by one, we climbed up on the platform and easily stepped over onto the camel. At the camel driver's command., the back legs of the camel stood up, and we grabbed hold of the saddle, fearful that we would slide off the front of the camel. Then the front legs stood up, and we were afraid we would fall off the back. Next, the camel driver led the camel on a 200 foot circular path and returned to the platform. The dismounting process was the reverse of the mounting procedure. Then the next person got on board. This was an unexpected highlight of the trip.

**

This was not my first camel ride. When I was in Cairo, Egypt several years before, part of the trip included a camel ride from where the bus dropped us off out to the pyramids and the Sphinx and back. However, a camel ride is always a thrill!

Puppetry

Puppetry is one of the strongest teaching tools in the world. People retain more information after a puppet show. Why? Because it stimulates two senses. If a person sees and hears a message, he will retain more than he would if he had just used one of his senses. Also, puppetry holds the attention of the audiences, especially children.

Also, almost any subject can be taught: the Ten commandments, moral issues, David and Goliath, Zacchaeus, Joseph and his coat of many colors, Jonah, the birth of Christ, arithmetic, spelling, history,…etc.

Now doctors and hospitals are using puppets to demonstrate to small children what is going to happen during a surgery they will have soon.

My friend Tom Spencer, after three medical mission trips to Ethiopia and retirement, became a puppeteer in 2003. His organization, which expands churches' efforts to spread the gospel by puppetry, is based on the theme of the Prayer of Jabez.

Tom started by teaching church women in Ethiopia how to make puppets and how to put on a puppet show illustrating a story or gospel message. By now, his work has spread to eight countries and some 200 churches.

In 2009 we went on a mission trip to Costa Rica. We made puppets to leave with the people there. We also taught them how to make puppets and taught them how to put on a show illustrating a certain point or telling a story, and gave them a chance to demonstrate and give a puppet show themselves, at their church service. They were so proud of themselves and gave a good puppet show.

We also gave them lots of material to make more puppets and gave them instruction books, patterns, and a DVD in Spanish about making and using puppets. We did this four times for women from 12 or more churches.

**

Costa Rica

Our mission team left an indelible mark on the lives of the people of the two towns in Costa Rica where we worked.

We held Bible School classes every day, during which we taught many lessons from the Bible and many Christian songs. Tom

Spencer taught the ladies how to make and use puppets, and we taught them how to give a puppet show illustrating Biblical stories and Biblical concepts, so they performed a good puppet show at their church service.

I had given them glasses with which to read the Spanish Bibles we gave them and to see to work again. We preached sermons in their churches. We gave them clothing and shoes. We did construction work enlarging their churches, we painted school rooms, and we enlarged a home. Essentially, we changed their lives.

In retrospect, the time of our departure from Costa Rica reminded me of Paul's departure from Ephesus as recorded in Acts at the end of Chapter 20. Those people cried and kissed Paul after he told them he would never see them again. They followed him to the ship and probably waved to him as the ship left.

In Costa Rica, when we were loading our buses to leave, the children, teenagers and adults crowded around and hugged our team members and wanted us to use Sharpie indelible markers and sign our names or a message on their t-shirts or on their bare arms. After some tearful farewells and kisses, our buses left for our hotel to pick up our luggage.

Ten minutes later, when we arrived at the hotel, we discovered that all of these children, teenagers, and many adults had used a shortcut and run over there. After much laughter, we had a second tearful session of saying goodbyes and hugs, and again had a t-shirt autographing party. As we finally drove off, they waved to us until we were out of sight.

**

After most mission trips, missionaries will experience similar farewells and goodbyes. Some are a little shorter, some a little longer that this one. These are experiences to be enjoyed.

Some churches like to go to the same town in the same country each year. They have developed special friendships with those people and help them each year. They also have found an in-country coordinator who has served them well in the past, and now they can trust him/her to take care of all the necessary arrangements each year for future trips.

Most church trips are sponsored by one church, or possibly two churches, and supply 80-90% of the team members. There are only a few vacancies filled otherwise.

About 30% of the team members attended Memorial Presbyterian, which planned and arranged for our Costa Rica trip. Seventy percent of the team came from other churches in our area, plus one or two from out of state. That church considered it a way to better serve people in the country we visited and to witness to those people about our Lord. This church also gave many others from other churches the opportunity to go on a mission trip and be trained to serve others and to witness to others about the Lord.

**

Camel Pulling Wagon in India

Chapter 13: Childhood Memories
About Missions

My father was an Indiana pastor. I grew up in a small town about 30 miles south of Fort Wayne, Indiana. There was a children's home on the outskirts of Fort Wayne which was supported by our church's denomination.

To give the children of that children's home a treat or summer vacation, many of the churches in our area asked their members to invite a child from that home to spend a week in their home during the summer.

Each family could match up their guest to their own children. For example if a family had two or three boys of a certain age, they could ask for a boy of that age. Likewise, if they had teenage girls, they could ask for a teenage girl.

Each child was picked up on Saturday and returned the next Saturday. Their children always looked forward to these weeklong visits. My family did too.

We always made sure we had an extra bike. We took our guest fishing for catfish. Winding by the outskirts of our town was the muddy, murky Wabash River, which was only a half mile away from our house. Like many kids, we skipped rocks on the water, seeing who could make a stone skip the most times. We also went rowing and fishing on our twelve-foot, old wooden rowboat.

Every spring the Wabash River, due to melting snows and heavy spring rains, would rise anywhere from eight to ten feet above normal and flood over the banks, covering all the surrounding fields and roads leading to the bridge with water. The river was filled with catfish and carp. Carps are some of the biggest, scrappiest fish around. We used worms and night crawlers for bait. If we couldn't find any, my dad showed us that sweet corn kernels would work just as well. The carp loved them.

Our boat was a twelve-foot, old wooden rowboat that had washed away from its owner someplace up river and finally became entangled in the trees and bushes near our home. When the waters receded back to normal, we found it and claimed it as abandoned property. No one ever came looking for it. It was our gift from heaven, and to us it was priceless. We chained it to a tree so that it wouldn't get loose again. We used it often during the summers. Before winter started each year, we would haul it up to our home on a small wagon and store it behind the garage.

Our guest from the children's home had never caught a large fish, and he was tickled pink. His biggest carp was just over 27 inches long. Big carp put up quite a fight for a boy who hooked them using a cane pole. When we walked home that evening, our guest had a great big happy grin on his face and enough memories in his heart to last a lifetime. We took pictures of him and his two biggest fish so that he would have bragging rights and could prove it when he returned to the home.

Sometimes we would take our guest and spend the day on a lake not too far away, where one of our church members had a cottage. We would fish, swim, and boat to our hearts' content. They also had an old, wooden log raft, which we poled or paddled around, pretending we were Huckleberry Finn.

Another day we would go out to a farm owned by a friend, and we would help with the chores--a big deal for us: we'd collect all the eggs in the hen house, help feed the cows at milking time, and feed the pigs. As our reward for all this hard work, we would be taken on a wagon ride out to the woods and back, pulled by a big farm tractor. What a thrilling, fun time we had!

In my childhood days, many homes had a porch which extended almost all the way across the front. Ours did. One of the best features of this porch was a large swing that could hold three people. It squeaked soothingly when it swayed just right. In the past, our mother had rocked her babies to sleep there.

Our guest had never seen a swing like that and enjoyed swinging on it, even in the rainstorms--if there was no lightning. Sometimes he would just disappear after supper, and we would find him out there, swinging away, with our dog sitting beside him, enjoying having his ears scratched.

Countless fireflies magically lit up that early July night sky. Fireflies blinking on and off like Christmas tree lights are the traditional symbol of summer to all kids. After dark, we would catch fireflies and put them in a glass jar and watch them glow on and off. One boy described fireflies as mosquitoes who are hunting us with flashlights..

At the church on Wednesday night, we would have a campfire, and each child was urged to roast his own hotdogs and marshmallows. The ladies of the church would serve us corn on the cob and watermelon. We each got our chance to turn the handle on one of the homemade ice cream churns, after which we were served a dish of that delicious homemade ice cream we had just made. What a treat.

It was great fun for my brother and me and for our guest. We learned a lot about getting along together and sharing. He told us what his life was like in the children's home, and we mentally compared it to the way we lived. We had never realized how fortunate we were to have loving parents. We really enjoyed these visits each year..

**

Another memory I have is the missionary speakers we had. Today, churches usually house these missionaries in a nice nearby motel or hotel. However, back in my youth, missionaries would stay overnight in the preacher's home. We had visiting missionaries whenever available, about two or three times a year. I remember that quite vividly because our guests always slept in my room, and I had to sleep on the couch. I've never forgotten that. However, it was worthwhile!

The missionaries would arrive Saturday afternoon and eat supper with our family. As my parents were talking with them, I would listen carefully. They told about what was going on in the country where they was serving. On Sunday morning I again listened intently as they told the church about their mission work and told amusing anecdotes.

They told of teaching songs and performing plays using costumes to illustrate incidents or stories in the Bible such as "The wee little man Zacchaeus who climbed a tree to see Jesus." Stories about David and Goliath, Jonah, Sampson, the Good Samaritan, and Moses were also popular. Illustrating the story always got the message across to the audience. Using puppets was another useful tool.

**

One of my uncles, Dr. Gilbert Schroer, was a missionary to Japan, and he could tell some of the most interesting stories I had ever heard. I often wished I could have been in Japan with him.

**

In March of my junior year at Ohio State, instead of going to Florida for wild parties during spring break--as many college students did, our college church youth group took a mission trip. Ten students in two cars visited and helped out at church orphanages, inter city centers, and at our church's nursing homes, colleges, seminaries, hospitals, etc. We even planted trees at one place. We learned much about church work during our visit to six states.

A year later, in March of my senior year, our college church youth group gave up our spring break to Florida again. We went on a second mission trip. Eleven students in two cars visited and worked at similar church facilities in seven different states and cities. We even painted rooms and did repair work. We talked to many people about church work during that week. Rev. Herb Muensterman was our youth pastor both years.

**

All these experiences served to whet my appetite for short-term missions trips.

**

Chapter 14: India

Growing up in the Midwest I could never understand the David and Bathsheba story in the Bible, where David looked out across the rooftops. All I was used to in the Midwest was steep roofs on buildings that had an angled pitch to drain off the rain and for the snow to slide off.

When I went to India, one evening we were invited to a dinner on our host's rooftop, and that story suddenly came to life before my eyes.

Many of the homes are long, narrow buildings with a staircase going up to the flat roof above. One day our medical team was invited to go to the home of one of the church members and eat the evening meal with his family.

When we arrived, we were ushered up the stairs to a nice open air space on the spacious rooftop. From there we could see the surrounding neighbors preparing their meals, children playing, and women weaving and doing other kinds of work. On the rooftop there was a refreshing, cool breeze.

Our host's brother was one of the co-hosts for our dinner. The next building over was his two-story home with a staircase leading higher up to that roof top. Since that was his brother's home, our group was invited to walk over to his home and climb the steps to see better. From the top of this taller building, we could see even more roof tops of the surrounding homes. We could see at least a football field's length away (three hundred feet) or more.

It was easy for us now to vividly visualize what David could have seen that fateful night in his life when he could not sleep. We can now understand how it could have happened.

Looking around later on, we saw that people on his two-story home next door were watching us also, probably out of curiosity and wishing that they could eat some of our dinner. We were watching them, and they were watching us.

**

After finishing our medical clinic one evening in India, we were waiting for our transportation. We saw a couple of big, black water buffalo oxen chained to a tree nearby. We walked over and admired their size and obvious power from about 15-16 feet away.

All of a sudden, the big bull charged directly at me, with his head down and his big horns pointed straight at me. I was so petrified that I couldn't move.

Fortunately for me, he hit the end of his chain and was stopped suddenly with a jerk, about a foot or two short of me. Trembling in fright, I backed up quickly and offered up a prayer of thanks for being saved from serious injury or death.

Possibly he thought I was infringing on his territory, and he was protecting his rights, or possibly he thought I was too close to the female oxen beside him, or perhaps he thought I would hurt him. Who knows why he charged me? I was glad to escape without injury.

I never want to do that again. After that close call, I had a much healthier respect for all of his 1,000 pounds or more of muscle and those two big, pointed horns.

**

On one medical mission trip to India, because of the lack of adequate facilities, my translator and I were off to the side from the rest of the team. All we had was a canvas awning above us for shade.

I had been working there ever since noon, and I had seen almost 200 people that day. There were about 40 more people to see, but it was starting to get too dark to see. There were about 100 pair of glasses on the table beside me.

Therefore, I announced through my translator: "It's getting dark quickly, and we can't see well enough to fit you any more. I will only see these next 10 people, and then we will have to stop. I'm sorry, we just can't see well enough."

A hush fell over the crowd.

Then with a yell, that whole crowd rushed forward and quickly grabbed all the glasses they could see and then fell back to see what I would do.

I just shook my head in dismay or disbelief, but I also felt a surge or relief, for I felt grateful that they had not hurt or injured my translator or myself.

We picked up what was left and went back to the rest of the group. Fortunately I had rationed out the glasses for the seven clinic days we would be there, and I had only taken that day's supply of glasses with me. The glasses for the rest of the trip were back at the hotel. It was so pathetic that they were so desperate for visual help that they would rob me of the glasses I was going to give them for free.

Following the 2010 earthquake in Haiti, the Haitian people have been so desperate that they, too, have been rushing forward and taking whatever they can lay their hands on. I have heard this from plane crews who have delivered supplies there.

**

At another clinic in India, we had very adequate facilities. Each doctor had his own room, and at the door to each room stood a doorman who only let in one person when one person came out.

To keep the patients moving quickly, we had 10 people in line inside the room about 15 feet away. When we finished with one person, he would head for the door, and we would start on the next person.

Sometimes when a new person entered the room, he would head to the front of the line and want to be seen next.

Of course the people in line didn't like that, so they would tell him to go to the back of the line. Sometimes pushing and shoving occurred if he tried to go only part way to the back of the line. This happened frequently. I assume it is a common practice for them.

Once, a lady came in, and she, too, went to the front and wanted to be seen immediately.

Of course, everyone else complained. However, she insisted that she had to be seen first because she had a sick mother at home to take care of.

I stayed out of it. I told my translator to take care of it. He knew his own people much better than I did. After a couple of minutes, they settled it, and she went to the back of the line.

I asked my translator how they settled it. He said, "One man said that her mother was not sick. He had seen her mother at the market place an hour ago. Only when her lie was revealed did the woman agree to go to the back of the line." How sad.

**

Before our group left for India, we were warned by our leader Reverend Ted Lott, that the streets of India are often dirty and are very crowded. Cattle, sheep, pigs, and goats wander around, either aimlessly or driven by a shepherd, sometimes leaving a trail of manure and urine. Chickens and ducks are plentiful also.

Three-wheeled bicycle pedal-powered taxis with a covered cab seating two in the rear are seen all over. Similar three wheeled taxis, powered only with a motor scooter engine, are even more numerous and more popular because they go faster. They hold up to four or five passengers. Taxi cars are also quite numerous.

Monks, priests and other workers from different religious groups attend our clinics because they desire or need the medical care or glasses we provide. We can tell who they are by their distinctive clothing or attire. Certain ones wear a very distinctive colored sash. They need help just like anyone else, or perhaps they are curious about Christianity and wish to obtain our Bible in their language so that they can read and study it. We gladly supply them.

Indian drivers drive like crazy and blow their horns incessantly. They speed around traffic circles avoiding or giving way to animals walking along. They run red lights by trying to get through every light that is turning yellow and then red. And yet, I seldom saw an accident or cars along the street that had been damaged in an accident.

Indian food is quite spicy, sometimes too spicy for certain people, yet just right for others.

Indian farmers grow very good crops, but the transportation of that food to market is a problem, and not adequate. Often vegetables that have been harvested and piled up are seen, waiting to be taken to market. The vegetables need to get to market before they get too ripe or spoil.

There is one type of car that has been made in India since 1945. That type of car--when made today--is identical to the first ones made. The manufacturers do not change it at all, and the parts made one year fit a car built 20 previously. This car only comes in two versions, a two-door and a four-door, and in just a few paint colors.

India has the second highest population in the world It is projected that India will surpass China in that statistic in another year or two. India also has hundreds of very fine colleges and universities, including some of the best in the world.

India has the second biggest movie industry in the world behind Hollywood--perhaps because making a film in India is far more efficient cost-wise than in the USA. The films and commercials which are produced there are excellent. Many of the actors speak fluent English. One of the sons of our in-country coordinator is an actor, and he worked with us several times when his schedule permitted.

**

India invites both compassion and curiosity, since millions of people are crowded into the cities in unbelievable poverty. And yet, amidst all this poverty stands the magnificent Taj Mahal gleaming with all its glory and splendor and white marble buildings

Over a billion people live in India. Some statesmen call it a poor country with lots of rich people, but to others, it is a rich country with lots of poor people. For Christians, it is ready for the harvest. Only three of every 100 people are a Christian.

**

COW PODS

While on trips to India, I noticed there were lots of cows, and I mean *lots* of cows.

Where there are cows, there also are lots of cow pods. For those of you not familiar with farm animals, I will just say that it is a pile of cow manure. Other animals such as horses, buffalos, musk ox, and others do the same.

When deposited by the animal, the pod is usually quite moist and falls to the ground and then often spreads out into a circular form about 10-12 inches in diameter and about 1-1 1/2 inches thick

Many people pick these pods up with shovels, load them into their carts or wagons, and take them to their fields or gardens and use them as fertilizer.

However, in India, wood is very difficult to find to make fires with which to cook. Some ingenious woman found out long ago that if a person lets the pods dry out, they make good firewood with which to cook. Good news travels swiftly; therefore, often a woman will be seen picking up these cow pods and stacking them neatly on top of a stone fence and letting the sun dry them out. Then, when they are dried out sufficiently, she will stack them neatly in some dry place and use them as needed to cook.

Sometimes the manure is in a tall, thick pile instead. I have watched women barehanded, dump this pile into a bucket of water, and then when it is soft enough, take it out and form it into a circular ring about 10 inches in diameter and then pat it down to about one inch thick. Then she puts it on top of a rock fence and lets the sun dry it. She does all of this bare handed.

Sometimes on mission trips, family at the place where the clinic is being held, will offer to serve lunch. Inside this family's courtyard will be seen dried cow pods stacked in a shed. Often, the family will serve fried chicken, fried yucca and/or fried plantains, and/or rice.

Before eating, with a smile on my face, I am always polite and grateful, but I also offer a silent prayer that whoever cooked the food washed her hands properly after handling the cow pods or chips--as some people call them--before touching the chicken to cook it. But I always wonder.

I also smile about the whole situation, because the chicken I'm eating may have been this family's pet rooster yesterday, but that was the only meat they had to offer me. I also keep in mind that what I'm eating today may have been what this family planned to eat tomorrow. Praise the Lord for generous, God-fearing people like that, who trust that the Lord will provide food for them tomorrow.

To describe the odor of burning cow pods is really quite a task, so I will leave that to your imaginations.

**

TAJ MAHAL

One year, after our mission to India was over, several team members decided to take a side trip to the Taj Mahal, which is about 125 miles south of New Delhi in Agar. Agar was the capitol of India in the 16th-17th centuries.

Emperor Shah Jahan had a harem with many wives. But when he met Mumtz Mahal, he was so enamored by her beauty and charm and fascinated by her personality, that he married her and ignored all the rest of his harem. He spent all his time with her.

The Taj Mahal is considered one of the seven wonders of the ancient world. It's beautifully proportioned white marble buildings and its symmetry is the same from all angles. Indian and Persian styles are combined into a single elegant form. Semi-precious stones are inlaid to form integral pietra designs. During the day, as the lighting changes, the Taj Mahal seems to look different. It is considered the world's most extravagant memorial to love.

Emperor Shah Jahan started building this lavish memorial on the banks of the Yamuna River, to commemorate his love for his beautiful wife Mumtz Mahal who died in 1629 while delivering their 14th child.

He hired the most prestigious architects and craftsmen in India, Persia, Iran, and Europe. It took 20,000 workers to complete it 22 years later in 1653. There is a reflection pool in front. Standing before it is exhilarating and awesome, more than words or pictures can describe.

A few years after it was completed,, the emperor was overthrown by his power-hungry son, who killed several brothers in a sword fight. Then he did to his father, the Shah, what *his* father had done to *his* father many years before. His father, the ex-Shah, was locked in a prison cell in nearby Fort Agra. Through his one and only window, all he could see was the lavish memorial built for his favorite wife.

The only imperfection in the Taj Mahal is that it was designed for one person. Since the Shah's death, his remains lie beside those of his wife. What a tribute to their love!

**

MARK

Mark Aliapoulios, one of our India team members, was from the Boston area. When we arrived back in Florida, he caught a flight to Boston, which arrived in Boston after midnight. There were no buses running to his area in the suburbs at that time of night. He had to take a taxi which would probably be quite expensive.

When a cab finally came at that time of the night, the driver did not get out. He just pushed a button which flipped open the trunk. Mark had to put his luggage in the trunk and shut it and then open the cab door and get in the cab.

He gave the driver his address, and then he commented, "I'm just returning from a mission trip to India, and I'm dead tired."

Actually, he was so tired that he dozed off to sleep. Pretty soon, the driver woke him up, by asking, "What exit do I get off?"

Mark told him and then added, "I'm so tired from my mission trip to India that I must have gone to sleep."

Finally, they arrived at Mark's house. The driver turned off the meter and turned and looked at Mark. The driver looked as if and was dressed as if he were from India.

The driver said, "You told me twice that you were on a mission trip to India. What city did you go to?" Mark said, "We flew into Madras, which is now called Chennoi, and then went by bus to the city of Guntur. Ever hear of that town?" "Yes," said the driver. "That's the town in which I used to live."

Mark said, "You speak very good English. How long have you been here in the states?"
The driver replied, "I learned English in school in India. I have been here in Boston for six months driving a cab."

Mark and the driver talked together for 25-30 minutes about India before the driver got out of the cab, opened the trunk, and got Mark's luggage out and set it on the curb.

The driver told Mark, "I turned off the meter before we started to talk, so I only have to charge you for the trip, not the time we were talking." Mark smiled, paid his fare, and gave him a good tip.

The driver thanked Mark for helping the people in Guntur, and said, "You go back next year! They need you! God bless you!" With a smile and a wave of his hand, he drove off.

Mark stood on the sidewalk realizing that God had intervened again to assure him that all the miracles and blessings of this trip to India really had happened.

**

Chapter 15: Why Am I Here on This Team?

Sometimes on a medical mission trip, someone will say, "Why am I here on this medical mission trip? I'm not a doctor, dentist, optometrist, nurse or a translator. I really am not needed on this team."

When I was on such a medical mission team to Mexico, I heard a man I'll call Joe, ask this question. Then Joe added, "I'm a mechanic at a caterpillar tractor dealership. What can I do to help this medical team?"

Our medical team stayed at a central location each night and then left by bus each day for a different small town an hour or two away, where we would hold our clinics usually inside a church.

On our first clinic day, our leader assigned Joe to be the driver of the medium-sized bus to take our team of 20+ members to our first clinic about 45 minutes away.

About halfway there, our stick shift bus stuck in first gear, and our driver could not shift gears. We were stuck miles from anywhere. Cell phones were not in common use then, so we were really stuck.

However, Joe, our driver, got out and crawled under the bus. Soon he shoved a wire up through the floor board. He had hooked it into the gear box, or linkage, or something else. When the motor was running, and the bus was moving slowly, he would pull up and down on the wire, and he could make the motor shift gears into second and then into third.

He took us to our first clinic assignment, and he drove us back to the base camp that evening after the clinic was over.

After supper that evening, the rest of us went to an evangelistic meeting. However, Joe stayed at the camp, and by lantern light and flashlight, he fixed the gear box or transmission, linkage, or whatever it was, and it worked fine for the rest of our trip.

In our opinion, Joe was the MVP on our entire team. Without him we would not have been able to go to the clinics. The Lord sent him along for that very reason. God hand-picked him because God needed a mechanic like him.

**

On another medical mission trip in Belize, we had two dentists as part of our team, and they had equipment for drilling and filling teeth We had known ahead of time that we would have electricity at each location.

At our first clinic location, everything worked smoothly, until about five minutes before closing time. Then the drill motor or the air compressor that runs the drilling equipment broke down and quit. Our dentists were dismayed and frustrated. They didn't know what to do.

We went back to the hotel where we were staying and ate supper at the restaurant.

Unknown to us, there was another medical mission team from Dallas, Texas, staying in our same hotel.

We got to talking to them and found out that they had a dental repairman with them who was asking the same question: "What am I doing here? I'm not a doctor, dentist, nurse or anything. Some lady back in Dallas paid for my trip, but I don't know why. I'm not doing anything."

When he heard about our dentists' problem, his eyes lit up. He told them that he was a dental repairman. He wanted to see their equipment. Soon he said, "I've got the part that is broken, and I've got the tools to fix it," and he did so.

In our opinion, even though he was from another team, he was the MVP on our dental team because he put our dentists back in business.

We got the name and address of the lady who paid for his trip and wrote her a letter telling her what had happened and thanking her for sending him. God knew why he influenced that lady to sponsor him on that trip. God hand-picked him for this trip.

**

When going on a medical mission trip to third-world countries, all members should follow these three extremely important rules:

Rule #1: Do not eat anything that has not been cooked, no fruit that has not been peeled.

Rule #2: Do not drink any water except bottled water or sodas. No exceptions.

If you do forget this rule, you are very likely to get dysentery or diarrhea.

Rule #3: When you leave the hotel or base camp each day, take some toilet paper or napkins with you. Practically all outdoor toilets do not have any paper at all. Many other toilets do not have any either.

**

I have been on several trips where one person, or several people, forgot to follow either the first or second rule and got sick and had to see one of our doctors. Also, they were not able to function very well for several hours or sometimes several days.

**

I was on another trip to Mexico, and one of our construction workers, a big husky fellow, forgot all three rules and had a bad case of diarrhea while he was out working one day. The only place available to him was an outdoor outhouse, with no paper. Guess what he did? He came out minus a pair of socks!

That taught him and the rest of us a lesson: be careful of what we eat and drink, and be prepared with extra paper.

Let me ask you a humorous question: "If you had a bad case of diarrhea on a mission trip as did the above man, and had to use an outdoor outhouse, with no paper, what would you do? Be honest with yourself.

**

A 12-year-old girl received her first glasses, a very strong pair of glasses for myopia, or nearsightedness. She looked out the window at some trees, and said, "I didn't know that trees have leaves! All I could see before was a big green blob." I would say that she was well satisfied, wouldn't you?

**

A 13-year-old boy had been told by his teacher to stay home from school because he couldn't see well enough to see and read the chalkboard.

After checking his eyes, we gave him a very, very strong pair of glasses (-14.00 for extreme myopia.) He looked around for several seconds, then he started smiling, and then his smile stretched into a big grin, and he said, "Now I can go back to school because I can see to do my school work again!" He was one very happy boy. He couldn't wait to see his teacher.

We gave him two pairs of glasses: One to use, and another spare pair to have in case he broke or lost his first pair. We also gave him an extra case to store his second pair in, so that they didn't get scratched.

**

Often the closing highlight of a trip is for the team, on the last night of the trip, to take their in-country coordinator with all the translators and other key personnel to a nice restaurant and recognize all of them for the help they have been. The coordinator and translators enjoy this very much--especially the recognition we give them, which encourages them to act as translators on another trip.

**

On one trip to a river town on a remote part of the Amazon River valley, we had three blonde girls, ranging in age from 18 to 25 years old. All the people in this town were black-haired, brown-skinned people of Indian background, with some Negro background mixed in.

The young men of this town claimed they had never seen a blonde girl before, and they all wanted to touch their blond hair and have their polaroid picture taken with these girls. The girls were flattered by this attention, and the rest of us were astonished by this type of curious interest.

Perhaps these three girls were on this trip to demonstrate the diversity of our world. God created all of us differently.

**

On a mission trip, if a song is being sung, and I don't recognize the tune or understand the language, I just smile and hum along softly and enjoy the melody.

**

It doesn't matter how much wealth we accumulate. It's how many lives we touch while here, that counts.

**

Even if we live near the ocean seashore and often stroll along the beach, we're not going to find a bottle with a message inside, telling us someone desperately needs our help in Haiti or some other country or island.

God doesn't work that way. God uses instant communication. God warned Joseph in a dream to take Mary and the baby Jesus and go to Egypt. They left immediately. Several years later God told Joseph in another dream to go back to Israel, and they left immediately.

Don't leave your footprints in the sand on a nearby beach, searching for a bottle. Leave your footprints helping people in need and giving them God's message of grace and forgiveness.

A wise man once said that living in a foreign country and learning the language of that country will increase one's knowledge up to ten times. That sounds true. This world is shrinking rapidly, travel-wise and communication-wise. North, South, East, and West need to share and learn to live together in harmony.

**

Chapter 16: Honduras Back-to-Back Trips and Bolivia

On another mission trip to Honduras, I took my wife because she speaks Spanish and because she wanted to go.

I had been to Honduras the year before, and also two years before that, so I knew the missionaries in Honduras well, and they knew me also.

I had arranged everything by mail with the secretary of the Dr. Baker with whom I had worked together the two preceding years. She had assured me that she would meet my flight and pick me up at the San Pedro Sula airport and take us to the missionary complex where we would stay. (This trip took place about two months after a major hurricane had devastated Honduras tremendously; therefore, a lot of people were desperate for help. Many had lost their glasses during the hurricane. Many had asked Dr. Baker if I could come and help them.)

When our plane arrived, and we got our luggage and cleared customs, I started looking for someone I recognized. There were four people I knew by sight because I had worked the past two years with them. An hour passed, and I still didn't see anyone I recognized, so my wife and I went to the information desk where my wife talked in Spanish to the people at the desk about our situation.

The lady said, "Since they have not come for you in an hour, I would suggest that you get a taxi and go to a hotel that is halfway between San Pedro Sula and the airport. That is a new hotel and very safe."

She continued, "Not all the hotels are safe since the hurricane. People are so desperate, they will break in and rob you, since you look like Americans, and they think you are rich. Also, you can not take just any taxi. Some of them will take you out to some deserted place and either kill you or else rob you and force you out of the taxi at gunpoint and leave you in the middle of nowhere."

"First of all," she continued, "let me make you a reservation at this safe hotel. Then let me find you a taxi driver I know you can trust."

Pretty soon she had made the reservation and found us a cab driver that she knew. She told him to take us straight to this certain hotel. We thanked her and gave her a generous tip for her help. When we got to the hotel, I was amazed at their security.

The hotel was brand new. The entire hotel was surrounded by a six foot high chain link fence, topped with a V-brace holding six strands of barbed wire on the top. There were two armed guards with repeating rifles at the one and only gate that was open at night. There were two more armed guards at the front door and more armed guards at the four corners of the hotel buildings. "Things must really be bad," we thought.

We went in and got our room.

Next, we looked in the phone book for my contact, Dr Baker, but there was no Dr Baker listed.

Since this mission station was supported by the United Church of Christ, we called up each church pastor for the Church of Christ listed.

My wife talked to them in Spanish and asked them if they knew Dr. Baker. On her third call, she found someone who did know Dr. Baker. That lady knew Dr. Baker quite well.
My wife gave her our phone number and asked her to call Dr. Baker and have Dr. Baker call us.

A few minutes later Dr Baker called us and apologized. Her secretary had had a death in the family, and she forgotten all about us in her haste to get a ticket and go home. Dr. Baker said she would come and see us in about 30 minutes.

A half hour later, she arrived with another lady. They assured me that all the plans for our clinics were ready and that they would come by and pick us up at 8:30 each morning for the rest of the week. They wanted us to stay at the hotel each night, because the night before at the missionary complex, one of the guards had been shot and killed at night.

We were cautious every day. Everything worked out fine. There were no problems at any of our clinics. All the people were glad to get glasses again so that they could see better. However, just to be safe, we were back inside the hotel before dark each day, and we ate there.

While driving through the countryside, we saw large cement culverts which had spanned small streams for the roadways and which had been pushed out into the fields by the force of torrents of water. Many other bridges were washed out, and a car had to drive down into the river bed or stream and then back up on the other side. It was hard to imagine that water could do that much damage.

Boy, was I thankful that my Spanish-speaking wife was along and helped us solve our problem. What a blessing she was on that trip.

Without her, it could have been a wasted trip. The Lord certainly knew what He was doing, when He encouraged my wife to go.

BACK-TO-BACK

In August 2003, I went on my second back-to-back medical mission trips. My wife doesn't like that, but nonetheless, she supported me. The group going on the second trip could not get an eye doctor to go and needed one badly, so I went.

On a Saturday afternoon, I returned from a trip to Peru. My wife washed my clothes, and I packed for my next trip. I checked my mail and emails. On Sunday morning we went to church, and immediately afterwards I drove to Miami with my wife and a friend. They dropped me off at the Miami airport and returned home. My plane left at 5:00 p.m.

The medical group I would be joining in Kenya, had left on Friday. I had shipped all my glasses with them. When I arrived in Kenya, I went through customs and started looking for my contact man. As usual, there was a multitude of people meeting that flight, all with a sign with someone's name on it. Finally, I spotted a man holding a sign with my name printed on it. I sure was glad to find him so quickly. He took me to meet the rest of the group, and the balance of the trip proceeded as usual.

When I got back from this, my second back-to-back trip, my wife cured me of ever doing that again. She greeted me at the door holding a strange small dog in her arms. We already had one small dog, and I could not understand why she had another small dog. She looked me in the eye, and seriously warned me, "I got this dog because you went on two mission trips back-to-back, and I was lonely. The next time you do that, I will get another dog." I could tell she was serious, so I never again went on two trips back-to-back. Three dogs is too many.

BOLIVIA

Our second medical mission trip to Cochabamba--the third largest city in Bolivia--was fully representative: doctors, dentists, an optometrist, nurses and support personnel.

On the second clinic day, a female Bolivian dentist stopped by and talked to the Bolivian hostess in charge of the clinic. Our hostess soon took the Bolivian dentist to our dentist.

The Bolivian dentist said, "I am a dentist, and I attend a sister church of this one, which is sponsoring your group. I would like to volunteer my services as a dentist and come in tomorrow afternoon and help you take care of patients.

Our dentist agreed. "Thank you. We'll see you tomorrow. Bring your equipment."

The next day, she arrived with her equipment at the proper time. Soon, she was working on one patient after another and was doing fine. However, with one patient, she was trying to extract a tooth when the top of it broke off at the gum line, leaving the bottom portion and the roots embedded in the jaw. (Dental training in many countries is far less comprehensive than in the USA.) She had never had this happen before, and she didn't know what to do. She had never been trained beyond basic procedures.

Totally frustrated, she showed her problem to our dentist, Dr. Mark Kuhl. He looked it over carefully and then said "While I take it out, I'll teach you how to do it, and then when it happens again, you'll know what to do." He could see her breathe a sigh of relief

Step by step, he explained to her what he was going to do, and why he did it that way. Then he did the procedure while she watched carefully. Finally, after several procedures, he removed all the rest of the tooth.

She thanked him for teaching her a new procedure in such a quiet, informative way that few people in the clinic knew that there had been a problem. Our dentist had followed the Golden Rule: "Do unto others as you would have them do unto you." Undoubtedly, in dental school, a professor had shown Dr. Kuhl how to correct that same problem, so now he was able to pass on that technique to another young dentist, saving her from what could have been an embarrassing situation.

Some medical mission teams are structured to conduct/ teach seminars in hospitals for the benefit of the hospital staff. In the above-mentioned case, our dentist was opportunistic and took advantage of a teaching moment when it arose with this Bolivian dentist

When we had seen our last patient for that trip, Dr. Kuhl gave the Bolivian dentist quite a few dental instruments which she didn't have, and that she needed for complicated cases such as the one described above.

Dr. Kuhl not only helped the people of Bolivia with their dental care that week, but he also taught a Bolivian dentist new procedures and gave her the necessary equipment to better help the people in the future. What a blessing and generous example he was to the rest of our team!

**

Our Bolivian team was fortunate to stay at the Bolivian Life Center Orphanage, which is home to 40 some young boys rescued from the city streets. Our vacation Bible study group held parties for them, played with them on the playground, and showed the love of Christ to them through hugs, smiles, new clothes, new shoes, and/ or long talks.

Sometimes the orphans talked about what their life was like before they were rescued from the streets and came to the orphanage.

Some stories were mind-boggling, some almost unbelievable about how they hunted for food in trash heaps, dumps, and behind restaurants. The bigger boys would take the food away from the smaller boys. They slept in cardboard boxes, old sheds, sometimes in old, abandoned cars.

Sometimes their family life had disappeared because of the death of one parent, sickness, drugs, or alcohol. Other children had been abandoned by their parents. Often, gangs of big kids would terrorize the smaller ones. They had the scars on their bodies to authenticate their report. Often, they were forced to deliver drugs and bring back the money. They almost starved, with not enough food.

The children were starved for attention. We ate with them several times and tried to learn all their names. We invited a clown to come over and entertain them. We held a clinic there one morning to be sure all the boys and staff members were in tip top shape.

Several older ones went with us to see the tall statue of Christ on a nearby mountain top.

**

On another note, in a very busy clinic, with 40-50 people standing in line to see each doctor, seldom can a doctor/ nurse stop his/her work and witness directly to one patient, because of the crush of other patients waiting in line for medical attention, all day long. It somewhat resembles an assembly line. Also, having to work through a translator takes twice as long, making it almost impossible for a doctor to witness, considering the backlog of patients to be seen.

We give each team member equal credit for each success story in the witnessing part of the entire clinic.

Chapter 17: Life is Full of Surprises

"Be Prepared" is the motto for the Boy Scouts. It also is a good motto for a mission trip.

Danger can be lurking just around the corner. Life is full of surprises.

For example, one day on one of my medical mission trips to the Ukraine, we were holding our medical clinic in a vacant office building which had an adequate number of rooms for our purposes. Each doctor, dentist, optometrist, and pharmacist had his own room, plus a large reception room.

Once we were assigned to our room, each of us hurried to set up so that we could start seeing patients. Unknown to me, there was an 18 x 24 square inch opening in the floor boards to the back side of the room, giving them access to the basement area below. Tools, equipment , extra chairs, and desks were stored below about eight feet down. This opening was covered neatly with boards the same color as the floor, but the boards were not nailed down.. It was not noticeable at all.

I weigh about 200 pounds. When I stepped back to inspect the way things were set up, I stepped on these boards and suddenly crashed through and in a flash found myself hanging hooked on one side of the hole with my right arm and elbow, and my left leg supporting me on the other side of this hole. I looked down into the hole and saw several pointed objects pointing up at me, and I shuddered to think what would have happened if I had fallen to the bottom. I uttered a thankful prayer to the Lord for His mercy.

Several husky fellows pulled me up to safety. One of our nurses checked my numerous scratches and bruises. The eye clinic was moved to another room, and others took over my job. I rested for the rest of that day. I was stiff and sore for days afterwards.

**

On a medical mission trip to the Amazon River in Brazil, one afternoon I started to feel dizzy and uncomfortable, so I told our leader, who suggested that I quit and go back to the boat . I packed up all my equipment and glasses, which one of the boat crew carried as he followed me back to the boat.

I started drinking Gatorade and other liquids and sleeping in my hammock. By the next morning, I felt much better and returned to my place in the clinic. I don't know if I was suffering from heat stroke due to a lack of liquids or what, but soon I was back to normal.

**

On my first trip to Mexico, We were on the island of Janitzo in the middle of Lake Patzcuara, holding medical mission clinics. Late in the afternoon, for some reason we had a short time when there were no patients in line to see us.

Therefore, Pastor Mullins, who was in charge of the group, invited two others and me to go over to a restaurant about a block away for a coke and some native pastry. We went and were back in about 20 minutes. I was feeling fine.

About 90 minutes later, when it was time to close the clinics, I packed up all my equipment and the glasses, ready to go. I was sitting beside the pastor, talking and eating some pastries. All of a sudden, without any warning, I passed out and slumped forward face down on the table. Needless to say, this caused a lot of anxious excitement and concern. A doctor rushed over and took my vital signs, but everything seemed to be okay.

Pretty soon, I came to and wondered what all the fuss was about. They asked if I had any heart trouble, and I said, "No." I told them that I had bleeding ulcers a few years ago, and that maybe that was what it was. The next morning, after a bowel movement with no sign of blood, I told the pastor and the doctors that it was not ulcers, but they were still uncertain about the cause. I think it was something I ate at the restaurant.

At the end of the trip, the pastor quietly told some of the rest of the people, "We'll never see him again." But he was wrong. I went with his group about ten more times, to Mexico and several other countries.

**

On one trip to Brazil, we were routed through Rio de Janeiro and had a seven or eight hour layover in Rio. We got a hotel room for the day near the beach. Our leader told us only to go out in groups, but always in two's at the least because of the pickpockets.

Most of us stayed in groups and had no problem, but one couple went out by themselves and walked along the beach. Waiting till there were no policemen in sight, a bunch of riffraff (beach bums) surrounded them and crowded around, snatching their cameras and binoculars and dispersed, running away in many directions so that they could not be followed. This couple was happy to get out alive. After this, they were grateful but also sadder but wiser.

**

On a medical mission trip to Ecuador, we stayed at a church camp at a lower altitude, but every morning we were bussed to a village up over 10,000 feet in elevation. Our clinics were held inside a building which had enough rooms for all the doctors, dentists, the optometrist, and a pharmacist.

On the last day of clinics, we were going to hold a church service immediately after supper and then go back to the base camp. So far, I had been doing fine, and I felt fine.

However, during the church service in that 10,000 foot high village, I began to feel cold. I was shaking and felt dizzy. With someone helping me, I got back to a car which took the others and me back to our base camp at a much lower elevation. Shortly before we got to the base camp, I rolled the window down and vomited several times. There were three or four doctors rooming with me in my room, and they decided that I had not drunk enough water for that high of an altitude. They gave me intravenous fluids for the rest of the night. By morning I was back to normal. I ate breakfast with our group, and we went home. Those doctors knew what to do in that situation and had the right equipment to take care of my problem, Praise the Lord.

**

I was on my way for a medical mission trip to Haiti, when we stopped at the island of Exuma in the Bahamas for fuel. As we were landing, I looked out my window and there off to the side on a small nearby hilltop below me was the wreckage of a DC-3 plane, just like the one in which I was flying.

After we landed, I found out that during a very bad, windy thunderstorm, a plane had lost power in one engine and could not maintain altitude and had crashed the week before on that island.

The pilot was to be praised for making the best of a very bad situation. Fortunately, no one was killed or seriously injured. All but one of the people on that flight were flown on another plane to Haiti the next day. As a precaution, one man was flown back to the states for x-rays. He had no broken bones, so he too flew on to Haiti.

All the usable equipment had been salvaged, and the owners were back in operation using other planes. Praise the Lord for his protection and mercy at that time.

**

On one trip to Mexico, our group was asked to hold a clinic in a nearby prison. Two doctors and I and several Spanish-speaking helpers volunteered to go

As we entered the prison, we were led into barred search cells with locked doors. We were searched and then taken to another cell, where the doors were again locked, and again we were searched.

It gave me a totally helpless feeling when I heard those doors clang shut behind me, and I knew that I was locked in. I couldn't help but imagine what it must be like for a criminal who knows he will be spending several years inside there, perhaps the rest of his life.

We helped the specific men who said they needed examinations The conditions inside the prison were very, very primitive with bare necessities.

Leaving the prison, we went through the same procedure in reverse order.

Perhaps if we let some of our stubborn, obstinate, hard-headed kids spend a night or two there, they might think about life differently and change their ways.

**

HUSBAND FOLLOWS IN WIFE'S FOOTSTEPS

Several years ago, a female doctor was in a terrible car accident which claimed her life and severely injured her husband.

She had often gone on short-term medical mission trips to developing countries. Her husband decided to continue her humanitarian efforts in her memory.

Since she was born in Ecuador, her husband set up a Medical Foundation to promote short term medical mission trips in Ecuador's poorer communities.

Her husband obtained the help of a civic Club in his hometown and now works in partnership with the same civic club in Quito, finding volunteers for these trips.

Doctors often do minor surgery and treat infections and wounds. Nurses do check-ups and parasitic control, they supply medical information, and they furnish medications. Visual needs are corrected with eyeglasses, and bad teeth problems are corrected by dental extractions.

To honor his wife's death, her husband follows in his wife's footsteps.

**

This reminds me of a another true story, which happened about 100 years ago, in the late 1890's to early 1900's. This is a story about a young missionary who set sail on a sailboat, before the advent of the steam boat. He was headed, perhaps for China or India. Back in those days, it took months to get to these countries.

However, this young man got sick on board this passenger sailboat and died. As Walter Cronkite used to say on his broadcasts, that's not the end of the story.

When the newspapers heard of his tragic and untimely death, they gave his story front page coverage. This story so inspired other prospective missionaries that soon about 200 more young men volunteered to go to the foreign country to which he had been headed and to take his place.

Those 200 that took this missionary's place probably accomplished far more than he by himself could have accomplished if he had lived. God multiplied his efforts 200 fold.

**

On a medical mission trip to the outskirts of Tegucigalpa, Honduras, we learned that another medical mission team en route to a certain nearby town had been stopped at gunpoint, robbed and forced to get out of their cars, and forced to walk back to town, while the bandits drove off with their vehicles and supplies.

Fortunately, no one was hurt, but that put a sudden stop to their trip.

Our prayers for protection and safety were heard. No such incident occurred to us, and our trip was a great success.

**

In Ethiopia, one day, a man with no legs drove up to one of our medical clinics, opened the car door, and dropped a small, wooden board similar to a skate board onto the pavement.

He got out and using arm power, sat on it. Pushing his hands on the ground, he moved into the building and told the receptionist he wanted to get some glasses.

We asked his age and found out that he wanted reading glasses. We tried several pairs on him, and soon he was beaming with joy and grinning from ear to ear. We gave him a Bible and he could see it, to read again. Now he was happy and satisfied.

**

In Ethiopia, a man came riding up to our medical clinic on horseback. He called out to some men who helped him off his horse. (He had been a very popular soccer player, who had injured his legs badly in an accident several years before that.) Now he needed medical help for a bad cold, and he needed glasses.

After seeing the medical doctor, getting cold medicine, getting glasses, and a Bible, he thanked us, had the men put him back up on his horse, and rode away. I never knew what to expect each day.

This reminded me of the story in Mark, Chapter 2, where four men carried a paralytic man to see Jesus, but they had to take him up on the roof, remove the tiles, and lower him down to see Jesus, and Jesus healed him. These men had to take this man off his horse, carry him to the doctors, and then carry him back and put him back up on his horse.

**

When the Russians controlled the Ukraine, they built large, theatre-type buildings, called palaces of culture, in many of the small towns in the Ukraine. They would seat perhaps 800-1000 people. They had a large stage at one end, which could be used for musical events, political speeches, orchestras, operas, bands, school assemblies, drama events, plays,...etc.

Twice, our group was allowed to use one. However, on one occasion, we thought we had permission to use one, but the orthodox priest had talked to the mayor, and we weren't allowed to use it. Only after some of our Ukrainian co-sponsors contacted some higher-up authorities, were we allowed to use it.

**

While in Bolivia, the Greyhound bus in which we were riding had a flat right, front tire.

Fortunately, it was not during rush hour, and the driver had room to get the bus off to the side and out of the travel lane. It was quite interesting to watch him change the tire. It just shows how having the right equipment and knowing what to do can make short work of a very intimidating job. Our driver made the change quickly, without much delay.

**

The place we stayed at in Nairobi, Kenya, was a church conference center with many one- room bungaloos. After eating in their dining hall one evening, part of our group was invited by a group of Kenyans staying there also, to come over at sundown, and watch their walking-on-fire ceremony. I think it was some kind of initiation ritual.

By the time we got there, a four-foot long bed of glowing, red, hot, fiery coals had been prepared behind some hedges in a secluded part of the conference grounds. While we watched from perhaps 15 feet away, about a dozen Kenyans participated in the ritual. Although we did not understand a word of their native chanting, we watched as each took off his sandals or shoes and walked barefooted across the fiery coals. No one cried out in pain or seemed to suffer any burns at all. We watched in awe and disbelief at this demonstration of bravery and being impervious to pain and burning. We shook our heads in amazement.

We don't know what the secret is. Some say that they step into a pan of cold water before stepping on the coals. Others say the trick is to keep walking and not stop on the coals. Others say that since the Kenyans walk around barefooted on rocky ground or on gravel roads, they develop such thick calluses on the bottom of their feet that they do not feel pain or burn their feet. Some say that they bathe their feet in some transparent heat-resistant chemical that they obtain from juices of some desert plants, which coats and protects their feet. Whatever their secret is, I'm not going to try walking across hot coals.

When my wife and I were in Fiji several years later, we saw a similar walking-on-fiery-coals demonstration. It was quite impressive also. I still don't know how this is done.

**

Inside a church in Cuba, our team was on the front platform, and the elderly pastor had just introduced us to his congregation. He stepped backwards and stumbled or tripped and fell backwards. Fortunately, he fell right into his chair, and thus was not injured . The Lord protected him.

**

On my first trip to India, we went to Chandigarh, a big city about two hours north of New Delhi by express train. We found out that an elaborate Indian wedding was going to take place at our hotel that evening. We were told that we could watch the preliminary part of it, if we stayed out of the way unobtrusively off to the side. That evening all the hotel doormen were dressed in full uniform and wearing pointed genie slippers.

The bridegroom was dressed in an exquisite black suit with a gold cape, wearing a gold crown with gold tassels. Carrying a sword, he came riding into the courtyard on a handsome brown horse with white stockings, seated on a highly decorated saddle and using a fine silver halter to guide the horse. He was followed by a dozen black suited bandsmen playing various instruments and holding up long bright lights.

Next the ladies were presented in lovely gowns, followed by the veiled bride in an elaborate beautiful gown. Soon dancing in the courtyard started , and then dancing in the street took place. Some of the young ladies in the watching crowd were invited to join in. Finally the entire wedding party moved into the banquet hall, and they closed the door on us. It was interesting to see.

**

India is famous for its tailors, who are excellent and quick. One morning at 7:30am many of our men went to a recommended tailor shop. We picked out the material we liked from their large selection. Their tailors carefully measured us up for suits. The ladies did the same at a nearby dress shop. Then we left for our day of clinics and evangelism.

At 7:30am the next morning we went back. We tried out our suits. They almost always fit perfectly. If necessary, they could make minor adjustments within a few minutes till they did fit perfectly. All this, for only eighty to a hundred dollars for a personalized tailored suit. We were delighted.

**

Along the Amazon River in Brazil, the culture is somewhat different. A nursing mother will just lift up her blouse and place the baby at her breast and nurse openly. It is so common place that no one pays any attention. I have seen it happen in church, while they are walking along, and several mothers kept nursing during their entire eye exam.

**

Doorman at Hotel for a Wedding

Spencer with Bridegroom at a Wedding

Chapter 18: Mexico, Dominican Republic, Haiti, and Cuba

A doctor and his wife, who is a nurse, were on one of our medical mission trips to Mexico, along with their two sons. The oldest son had just graduated from high school and would go to college in the fall. His brother had just finished his sophomore year in school and would start his junior year in in the fall. Neither boy had much of an idea of what his parents did at work each day and had not wanted to go on this trip. Their parents had made them come along.

After arriving at the base camp in Mexico that day, we unpacked and ate supper. When it started getting dark, we had a campfire meeting. We were seated on logs forming a big circle about 50 feet in diameter around a blazing log campfire in the middle.

First, we were told our plans for the next day, and then we were instructed to one by one stand up, tell our name and state, and tell what we wished to do on this trip. For example, the first person stood up and said, "I'm John Tucker. [Names have been changed in this story.] I'm a dentist from California, and I will take care of the dental problems of all the people I see each day."

Finally, it was the doctor's oldest son's turn. He stood up and said, "I'm Tom Murphy. I didn't want to go on this trip at all. I wanted to stay home and play soccer with my friends. My parents forced me to come on this trip." A poignant hush fell over the group.

Next his brother stood up. "I'm Bill Murphy, Tom's brother. I didn't want to go on this trip either. I wanted to stay home and play soccer and ride my bike. My parents forced me to go on this trip, too." Again, a total hush settled on the group for 10-15 seconds.

The next young man stood up and said, "I'm Joe Barnes This is my second trip to Mexico. Last year I enjoyed helping the people here so much that I came back this year to help them." A round of applause greeted his words.

After the entire circle of introductions was completed, the doctor stood up and said, "I apologize for what my two sons said. Their mother and I thought it best if they go on this trip and see how the other half of the world lives. We thought it would do them good."

I don't know what their parents said to those two boys, if anything, but I feel certain that both parents were very embarrassed.

I'll have to give those boys credit, though. At least they were honest about their feelings. Also, every day for the rest of the week, they pitched in and did what they were asked to do. They rolled up their sleeves and got dirty working. They washed feet, took blood pressures, helped disabled people get up the stairs to the clinic, and watched their father and mother helping the sick and injured. They held babies while the mothers were being seen and watched their father put a cast on a boy with a broken arm.

They watched the dentist working on teeth and saw several teeth-- which were too rotten to be repaired--extracted. They watched the optometrist give people glasses and saw how happy the people were when they realized they could see well enough to go back to work and support themselves again.

We had another campfire after our last clinic day, and the two sons stood up and apologized to their parents. The oldest son apologized to the group saying, "I really didn't know what my father as a doctor and my mother as a nurse did each day. I now realize how much these people need help. I want to go to college and be a doctor or nurse like my parents. I thought to myself, "What a difference a week makes! This trip has been an answer to their parents' prayers for them.

**

On one medical mission trip to Mexico, I was leaving a day earlier than the rest of the team. That morning, the leader of our group hailed a taxi and told the driver to take me to the airport about an hour away. Pastor Tom Mullins paid for the trip, and I got in.

I had to sit in the front seat with the driver because the back seat was filled with a man taking crates of chickens to the market. Many other crates of chickens were strapped on top of the taxi. We drove to the marketplace where the man and his chickens got off.

Then we headed for the airport. On the way there, a big brown dog dashed out and got in front of the taxi and was run over. To this day, I still remember hearing that dog yelping in agony and seeing the blood gushing from his mouth as we drove on. Every once in a while, when I see Pastor Mullins who put me in that taxi, he kids me about the chicken taxi ride.

One time when he introduced me to the whole church, Pastor Mullins told his congregation about watching me ride off with all those chickens on top of the taxi. It must have been a hilarious sight. He grins every time he thinks or talks about it.

**

I grew up in a small town, and back then, people living on the outskirts of town had some chickens for eggs and often raised fryers in the summers. Therefore, I was familiar with roosters.

Their early morning crowing announces the beginning of a new day. They also crow anytime they feel like it, and they don't care what day it is.

I have always been fascinated with the story of Peter's triple denial. Jesus had predicted both it and his subsequent repentance. That moment in time, when the cock crowed thrice, Jesus looked Peter in the eye as he denied Jesus for the third time. This defined Peter for the rest of his life. He rushed away and wept bitterly, but he repented and decided to trust Jesus. He did not become another Judas. Out of our failures, God can get our attention and humble us. Then we can go on to some of the greatest successes in our life.

Every time we hear a rooster crow, we should be reminded of this story and be sure that all our decisions honor the Lord in everything we say and do. I feel sure Peter remembered that moment forever, whenever he heard a cock crow again. We need to trust Jesus too. Frequently on mission trips, I've heard roosters crow. I enjoy it, but I also remember that it was Peter's wake-up call.

In July 2005, I went on a mission trip to Santiago, Dominican Republic with a Spanish-speaking church, Oasis de Amor, which my Cuban born wife, Anna, had helped start about 22 years earlier at Gold Coast Baptist Church in WPB. God had blessed and multiplied the efforts of the beginning group of people. Over the past 15 years, under the dynamic leadership of their young pastor, Reverend Daniel Casanova, they had grown into a congregation of almost 400 members and moved into their own church building.

We landed in the capitol, Santo Domingo, and then started on a several hour trip on a Greyhound type bus to Santiago. Halfway there, our bus broke down and stopped.

The driver called back to their office and asked for a replacement bus. A couple of hours later, it arrived, and we proceeded on to Santiago.

Our medical team consisted of myself, several nurses checking blood pressure and for worms, and several helpers. All of the team were bilingual, except for me, their English only member.

Oasis de Amor had been on a mission trip to this same church in Santiago several times before and had developed close friendships with many of the members of that church. They corresponded together frequently.

When our American church announced that they were going to Santiago in July 2005, one prosperous, engaged young couple set their wedding date so that it would take place while we were there and invited our entire group to their wedding. This Dominican-style wedding and reception was a very enjoyable and unexpected highlight of our trip.

**

Some people want to take off their shoes and wear sandals as Jesus and the disciples wore, in order to know what it was like to walk as Jesus walked. Some want to walk a long distance on a hot day and smell the sweat of the rest of the group as Jesus did. Others want to sleep under the stars as Jesus did, or fry fish on a charcoal fire as Jesus did in John 21:9.

Basically, Christianity is about whom you know personally.

**

On a mission trip to Haiti, I noticed that one lady did not seem interested in seeing better but was more interested in getting the best-looking frame available. I had checked her distance vision, and she saw 20/20 with each eye. She was over 50 years old, so I knew that she must need reading glasses. I tried a +150, then +200 and then +250, but nothing helped her see better. She kept saying, "No good" to everything I tried. Finally, I asked her, "With which one can you see the best?" She then pointed to the good-looking gold metal frame. So as a test, I tried that good-looking frame on her. In my opinion, the lenses were much too strong for her. They had a +700RX in it. She said, "That's good. I'll take this pair."

I seriously doubted her and before I gave them to her, I asked the local pastor about her strange request. He told me, "There is a flea market nearby that is open on Saturdays, and it has some very good items for sale sometimes. Perhaps she knows what items sell over there and expects to make some money that way."

This was not the way I had expected to help the people of Haiti, but I decided that if she was that smart and had that much ingenuity to figure out a way to get some money, I would give them to her and let her raise her financial status that way. What would you have done?

**

Haiti and the Dominicn Republic are two countries that share the same island. Haiti occupies the western third of the island, and the Dominican Republic owns the eastern two thirds. Both have lots of mountains in certain areas. The Dominican Republic has far more tourist trade. Haiti is very poor, having depleted its forests to make charcoal with which to cook.

I was very fortunate to have missionary friends in both Cap Haitian in Haiti and in Santo Domingo, and I could stay with them in their homes, which was a safer choice than the hotels. Sometimes people are robbed even in a hotel. I worked twice in the La Romana-Higuey-El Seibo area, twice north of Santo Domingo in the sugar cane towns, and one year in the northern highlands area at Santiago, Dominican Republic. The people in both countries are very grateful for the help we give them.

**

Christopher Columbus landed on both Dominician Republic and Cuba. I have seen a casket in Santo Domingo which is believed to hold his remains. However, Cuba claims they have the right casket with his remains. Spain also claims they have the right one. Who knows which is right?

**

A Pastor in Cuba had his car stolen about a week before we got to Cuba. He got his car back the day we arrived. Two days later, we were scheduled to meet him at a meeting.

He was driving to meet us when the police stopped him for driving a stolen car. He was put in jail for several hours before he could convince the police that he was the owner of the car. The police had not updated their records, and the car was still listed as stolen.

All three countries are interesting to visit, and all their people are friendly and kind. Each has its own interesting history and points of beauty.

**

Cuban streets have many American cars, vintage 1940, 1950, 1960, models of all kinds.

They are still running. It's like an antique car rally. The mechanics are quite ingenious and can take a carburetor or distributor from a 1940 Ford, for example, and make it fit in a 1970 Plymouth, a 1960 Chevrolet, a 1950 Buick, or a 1965 Cadillac.

Cuban auto body workers also are very good and can make a new fender out of damaged parts. Many of the cars must be running after 600,000 or 700,000 miles It's unbelievable. There are some new Russian cars, and some new Japanese and German cars also.

In Cuba, religious talk is not allowed on streets--only in church or at home.

**

Chapter 19: Who Says You Can't Live Life a Second Time?

I am a pair of bifocal eyeglasses. Who says you can't live life a second time? Listen to my story.

My first owner was Philip Schroer, a 46-year-old man of German descent who lived in West Palm Beach, FL. Before I met him, he had attended high school and graduated from college with a Master's degree and had served as a pilot in the USAF. He married his college sweetheart and they had four children: two boys and two girls.

Highly interested in physics and mathematics, he was motivated to pass on this knowledge to the next generation, so he became a high school teacher for over 40 years.

When I met him, Philip was 46-years-old and having trouble with his near vision. He had gone to his optometrist, who prescribed bifocals, and suddenly I was created for him.

I was his second pair of glasses but his first bifocals. I helped him see the newspapers and magazines. I helped him prepare his lessons for school and look through reference books at the library. He read a lot of books.

I helped him with his golf game and made sure he made contact with the ball. I helped him coach freshman basketball at the high school. Through me, he watched his college team win the Rose Bowl. Man, was he thrilled to see that! Through my lenses, he has seen several graduations, holiday gatherings, weddings, vacation trips, and babies' first steps.

Best of all, I, as his trusty bifocals, enabled him to see the interest in his students' eyes as they listened to his explanation of the scientific wonders of this world in which we live.

He told them they could enjoy the best of it if they studied hard to learn as much as possible. He was a very successful and much admired teacher and earned many awards for his work of disseminating knowledge to thousands of students.

I helped him see the happiness in his children's faces during various activities, sports and trips, for he believed in spending time with his children, who enjoyed his wit and humor.

Sadly, my life with Philip only lasted four and a half years. He started having near vision problems again and went back to his optometrist. Dr. Meckstroth prescribed stronger bifocals; therefore, my first life came to a sudden end.

Fortunately for me, Dr. Meckstroth had a box at the reception desk of his office with a sign which read, "Please donate your old glasses to help the needy overseas." As Philip reached the desk to pay his bill, he saw this box and paused for a few moments.

I was praying hard all the time: "Please drop me in the box so I can help someone else. I don't want to be shoved in a drawer someplace and become forgotten and useless." God touched Philip's heart, and his generosity prompted him to drop me in the donation box. Dropping me into the box, he said, "This has been the best pair of glasses I ever had." I breathed a sigh of relief, for now I would soon be helping someone else.

Dr. Meckstroth was a golfing buddy of Philip, so after Philip left the office, he retrieved me from the box and put me in a special, bright orange case with Philip's name on it.

Every Saturday, Dr. Meckstroth would empty out the box, clean and mark the glasses power wise, and prepare for his next mission trip. I was in great shape, no scratches or anything. I was usable and passed his test. Unfortunately, some of the other glasses in that box were not so lucky. Others were broken, scratched, or missing a lens,…etc. Those glasses were discarded, and that was the end for them. I realized I should thank Philip for taking good care of me.

Two months later, still in my orange case, I was packed with about 1,000 other glasses into three suitcases, and we headed for the mountain town of Andahuaylas, Peru in South America, where Dr. Meckstroth had been the previous year.

I was thrilled to be going to meet my new owner and hoped to serve him as well as I had served Philip.

It was cold in the mountains at that elevation on this, the third day of clinics. After the usual tests, I was picked up with two other pairs. The man was asked, "With which pair of these three do you see the best?"

He tried on the pair that was a trifle weaker than my Rx. Then he tried me on. And then he tried on another pair that was a trifle stronger than my Rx.

My heart jumped with joy when the man said happily, with a big grin on his face, "I see much better with the second pair. It's the best."

Now I had found my second owner, and so I started my second life.

With me, this man could now see fine at distance and could read even the smallest size of print.

A 47-year-old man, Alberto Sanchez, is married and has six children. The oldest three are married. He earns 3,900 sol each week, slightly less than 10 U.S. dollars. He works in a furniture and carpentry shop. His job had been in jeopardy because of his diminishing near vision, but he couldn't afford to see an eye doctor for a pair of glasses.

Dr. Meckstroth took a picture of Alberto wearing his new glasses, and another with him and his wife and three younger children. Afterwards, Alberto was so happy that he went outside and told all the people that were waiting in line to see a doctor how satisfied he was with his new glasses. Language was no barrier. I understood both English and Spanish.

About two weeks after the trip ended, Dr. Meckstroth gave Alberto's pictures to Philip as a birthday present. Philip was delighted to learn that his old glasses could change Alberto's life so much.

Philip's old glasses are working hard to serve his new owner. His glasses are happy to be useful again. Who says you can't live life a second time? Recycled glasses do.

Chapter 20: The Composition of a Medical Mission Team

Most of my mission trips have been medical mission trips. I am an optometrist, so that is where my training and skills fit in the best.

I have been on 11 wonderful trips with Christ Fellowship, on 8 trips with First Baptist, WPB, on 7 trips with Goldcoast Baptist, and on 5 trips with Greenacres Baptist, all from here in Palm beach County. They all have well-organized, interesting trips, reach many people, and keep their mission teams busy.

I have been on seven wonderful trips with AMOR (Amazon Mission Organization) and that has been a different kind of experience, since we travel and live aboard a double deck 78 foot boat that formerly was a river freight boat. Revamped now, it is quite comfortable as we get to sleep in hammocks. Headquartered in Manaus on the Amazon River, this group offers 8-10 trips each year. These 10-11 day trips feature medical mission teams, plus Bible school, preaching, and construction teams.

I have been on five wonderful trips with VIMM (Volunteers in Medical Missions). I heartily agree with their director, Larry Secrest's description of their recent work:

"Our medical outreach affords believers the opportunity to put their faith to work and to display the reality of the gospel by offering medical services to needy people."

I have also been on three wonderful trips with the Tampa Bay Baptist Association. They plan good, multifaceted trips. We stay quite busy and see many people, which is good.

I have been on a number of multifaceted trips, which besides the medical team, also feature one or more of the following: a preaching/ evangelism teams: a drama team, a Bible school team, a construction team, a sports team, a singing team, and a puppet team.

I have enjoyed each and every trip with these various groups and churches.

Team Composition

Often a typical multifaceted medical/construction/bible school mission team is composed
of

1-3 medical doctors
1-2 dentists
1 optometrist
1 pharmacist or pharmacy student
4-5 nurses or nurses aids
1-2 preachers
4-6 Bible school teachers
2-4 construction workers or possibly
10-12 skilled workers
6-8 translators (they might come with the team, or they might be hired or volunteer)
The in-country liaison person should have the translators firmed up and definitely committed to working before departure for the trip. Translators are extremely important.

The in-country coordinator must have the proper transportation, drivers, housing, food, publicity, clinic times, arrangements, and deposits made ahead of time, if necessary.

All of these items should be checked 10 days before departure, and the day before departure.

It is extremely important to have a trustworthy person make the necessary preparations at the place that is going to be served. This person should be given a check-list of things that need to be done and ready for the visiting team. I have been on two trips that started out badly when we arrived at the airport, but with ingenuity, everything worked out. However, if we had had a very large group, that arrived late at night and had found no transportation ready or housing available, it could have been disastrous.

**

A multifaceted team might include all of the above, but some teams are smaller and more specific: dedicated to one or two objectives.

One time on a medical mission team to the Ukraine, we had seven medical doctors, one optometrist, and five nurses. This was a very medically oriented trip, plus we distributed free Bibles.

On another trip to India, we had eight preachers, one optometrist, and two nurses. We were top-heavy with preachers because we preached at eight churches on Sunday morning, at another four churches on Sunday afternoon, and at eight different churches on Sunday evening. On weeknights, Bible studies and services were held in many churches also.

Another team I was on had two dentists, two optometrists, and two helpers plus two volunteer translators we met when we arrived. We only served people with dental or eye problems.

A medical mission team can be a small group, medium sized group, or as large as 30-40, depending on facilities for housing, a place to hold clinics, transportation, food, and publicity,...etc. The availability of key personnel in each desired category is also a big factor. Sometimes a team would like to have a certain specialist but can not find anyone willing to go at that specific time. I recommend that the team be flexible and go without this person. He may come the next year.

Several Christian colleges or universities offer mission trips for their students.
Sometimes non-students with certain skills are allowed to go to broaden their scope of impact. I have gone with Palm Beach Atlantic University and Belmont College from Nashville, TN.

Other times a team will be sponsored by a Christian medical organization, like VIMM, which organizes 12-18 medical mission trips each year. In January each year they publish in their monthly newsletter the dates and places to which they will be sending teams. All participants of their past trips are thus notified, and they can sign up for the trip they wish to go on or tell other interested people about the availability of such trips. Such trips usually have quotas as to how many doctors, nurses, dentists,...etc. that they need, so reservations need to be made early. Often, a team of 20-25 like this will have team members from many areas or states.

**

Mission trips are not for everyone. All team members should be Christ-like in their actions, words, and deeds at all times. Some teams have a written code of conduct agreement for each member to abide by and sign.

I have been on mission trips during which we've experienced problems with disruptive behavior, getting into fights, knocking down doors, breaking windows, being a practical joker and spraying a teammate's bed with liquid detergent, not paying attention during worship services, drinking, and smoking. All applicants under the age of 18 and their parents need to be told upfront that these types of behaviors are totally unacceptable. Missionaries need to be Christ-like at all times.

Also, if the applicant has a history of getting quite homesick and might insist on going home early, that is a factor that needs to be evaluated. Rescheduling tickets may be costly.

ARE YOU BEING WATCHED??

A wise man said, "Always remember that your children are always learning from you and watching you, so do your best to be the adult you want your children to become."

Children will copy their parents' vocabulary, actions, and mannerism. They will even walk like their parents. Children listen to their parents, but if the tone of the parent's voice gets too loud/strong, the children will tune that voice out.

When a person is on a short term mission team, the patients he sees each day are watching; listening; and judging facial expressions, frustrations, and sarcasm,...etc. all the time. They watch how missionaries handle perplexing situations. Some may speak more English than the missionaries realize. Therefore, missionaries need to be extremely careful about what they say and do. Missionaries should try hard to be as kind and understanding as they can be, as Christ-like as they can be.

**

Many churches, groups, and organizations that sponsor and plan mission trips expect the trip teams to give them a report about the trip a few weeks after the trip is over.

Often people who have helped pay for this trip expect the same courtesy.

Some mission groups area composed of multifaceted teams. There may be a medical team, a construction team, a Bible school team, a preaching team, a puppet team, a music team, a drama team, and/ or a sports team.

A group may have some teenagers, some women with small children or babies at home, young married couples, middle aged people, or retired people over 65.

Often, when each of these different people or groups give their version of the trip, it is colored by their interests.

Sometimes, to get the best possible overall report on the trip, perhaps a composite report from each person or team represented would be best.

Chapter 21: Chasing a Dream? Air Travel and Saint Paul's Travels

After listening to D.L. Moody at a meeting one evening, someone came up to him and said, "I don't like your way of witnessing. It's not very effective."

D.L. replied, "I like my way of witnessing much better than your way of not witnessing at all." The man had no answer to that and silently turned away. Too many people are like that. So critical of others' work but doing nothing themselves.

Some people are couch potatoes. They go to church almost every Sunday and listen to the preacher talk about following Christ's last commandment: "Go and preach the gospel all over the world and baptize in Jesus's name," as recorded in Matthew 28. They have heard missionaries, home on furlong, telling about their activities and their needs. They have seen pictures of the missionaries' work, but they just sit there totally unresponsive, basking in the glory of their inertia.

One of these days, if the blood in their veins has not solidified by then, when a close friend, or a family member, or someone they look up to, returns from a short term mission trip, their transformation will begin. They will listen to the missionary and see him at work in the snapshots of his mission trip. After seeing him in the pictures and listening to the tone of excitement and enthusiasm in his voice, these people will become inspired to go also.

When this friend tells them about another short term mission trip that he is going on soon and about the need for several more team members, these people will suddenly decide to go, since they will now have a friend on the trip.

Once they've decided to go, all it will come down to is putting one foot in front of the other, as they go down the check list of things they have to do in preparation for their trip.

Basically, in the past, all of their reasons for not going were nothing more than a form of praise. Missionaries were doing something they wanted to do but weren't brave enough to do.

Soon these people will have that dreamy look in their eyes, the kind one experiences after he's traveled to and from faraway countries.

Does that mean that everyone should go on a short term mission trip? Not at all. If a person can not walk at least a half mile without stopping to rest, or if he has certain medical problems, he should see his doctor first. Persons who *can* physically can go on a short mission trip should pray about it. God will either lead them to go on a mission trip or not. Certainly, God calls some people to do missionary work right in their home town.

Also, God may call some persons to donate money so that someone else can go. Those that donate money should ask the missionary they are supporting to provide a full report and take lots of pictures so that they can vicariously live their adventures and experiences through the missionary.

Most people who go on their first short term mission trip return saying, "I'm sorry I waited so long."

AIR TRAVEL

On some mission trips, we have several types of travelers: some are on their first airplane ride and looking forward to it. Others are extremely fearful of flying, evidenced by their closed eyes, clenched white fists which alternately grip the magazine they had nonchalantly been pretending to read and then their shirt sleeve. Others have never been out of the USA and are wondering if they will get sick, or if everything will work out smoothly.

There are also the seasoned travelers who have flown many times to many different places.

For those that haven't flown for year or two, I'm going to do some reminiscing about it. First, the passenger boards the plane and takes his seat, and soon the plane is ready to depart.

Then he hears, "Welcome aboard. Thank you for flying [our airline] today."

He looks down at the magazine pocket in front of him and checks if the airline magazine is something he wishes to look into later.

Looking around, he may speculate about his fellow travelers' occupations and their reason for today's flight. The man beside him may be on his way to visit his newest granddaughter. The young soldier across the aisle may be returning home from a war zone. The good-looking young lady two rows ahead of him may be a model en route to a new assignment. The man in front of him is working on his computer and may be on his way to an important seminar. The woman in the aisle seat one row ahead of him might be a salesperson going to a convention. The older couple behind him may be returning from a vacation.

Below him in the belly of the plane is a huge cargo space. All sorts of items are being shipped: mail, time-sensitive legal documents, fresh flowers, fish from South America, motors from Detroit, museum artifacts and displays, sometimes even a mummy or two, computer parts, perhaps a precious human organ shipped in a refrigerated container to a surgery center to save a life in need of that organ. The list goes on and on.

Today's airline cargo capabilities have expanded tremendously since back in 1926 when the famous Charles Lindbergh flew his small plane that only carried passengers and mail.

Modern day jets have expanded mission trips drastically. Now teams can travel long distances to far-away countries in just hours with all their supplies and equipment. Then they return after a week at their mission place. The Apostle Paul on all his trips, did not travel like this at all. All his travel was on foot, donkey, cart, wagon, or a sailboat. Also, he had to carry all his belongings, blanket, and food in his backpack. Since he was a tentmaker by trade, he probably carried a tent for shelter.

The Apostle Paul

Paul personally went from city to city in many countries. Paul's eloquent preaching about Jesus and daily counseling with the people in cities he visited on his numerous trips spread the gospel. All his preaching about Jesus, his personal contacts, and his letter writing of instruction and encouragement to all these people sent out Christian ripples which spread throughout the then-known world, causing many people to become Christians. He wrote the book of Romans, from which we get the "Roman Road" or the "Highway to Heaven."

The book of Acts give us a good description of Paul's four journeys:
Chapters 13-14 cover his first trip.
Chapters 15-18 cover his second trip.
Chapters 18-21 cover his third trip.

Chapters 22-26 cover his trials and problems around Jerusalem for two years.

Chapters 27-28 cover his fourth trip, which was to Rome.

Using Biblical maps of his four trips, and (1) assuming that the scale of miles for these trips is accurate, and considering (2) measurements are made *as a bird flies*, not the way the roads zig zag around, and curve around rivers, lakes, peninsulas, and mountains etc.

Therefore I estimate that Paul traveled:
  On his first trip-----------1,500-1,700 miles
  On his second trip------- 2,300-2,600 miles
  On his third trip--------- 2,600-2,900 miles
  And on his fourth trip--- 1,600-1,800 miles (one way to Rome).
Total distance traveled---8,000-9,000 miles.

Using modern jets, Billy Graham, for example, traveled much farther than that *each way* in less than 24 hours, when he left his home in North Carolina and held a crusade in Sidney, Australia or in Tokyo, Japan, or in Calcutta, India.

More Recent Evangelists

There are many other great missionaries or evangelists who followed in Paul's footsteps:

John Knox. Ulrich Zwingli, Martin Luther, John Calvin, Jonathan Edwards, Dr. David Livingstone, John Wesley, Charles Wesley, Charles Spurgeon, John Wycliffe, Dwight Moody, Billy Sunday, C.S. Lewis, Louis Palau, Billy Kim, David Jeremiah, John Hagee, Charles Stanley, Franklin Graham, Joel Osteen, and many others.

One of the very best is William Carey of Scotland. He wanted to go to India, but no one would support him. Finally, he raised the money and went to India in the 1800's. He worked tirelessly and won hundreds to the Lord. He is known as the "father of modern missions."

He trained many young men to become native pastors. He translated the Bible into 40 different languages spoken in India. When he died, I feel certain he heard these words from the Lord: "Welcome home, you good and faithful servant, you have accomplished what you were sent to do."

Another of the best missionaries is Billy Graham, who, in 1949, came into national prominence with his two month, highly publicized Los Angeles crusade. Of the 300,000 attendees, 6,000 were converted.

After that, Billy Graham has preached to over 100 million souls in over 80 countries and in every state in the USA and on all six continents. By preaching face-to-face to over 100 million people at his world-wide crusades, he has changed the lives of millions of people.

By now, with new advances in TV, satellite, and radio broadcasting, it is estimated that he has reached well over two billion people.

Chapter 22: Sightseeing, Souvenir Shopping and Translators

While on many mission trips, the last half day, or even the last day, is often devoted to shopping and/or sightseeing. That is a good idea to broaden the team members' knowledge about the country in which they worked. Everyone will be better equipped to tell others about the trip and to show others the handicrafts of that country. Sometimes the members of the mission team will wish to buy a present for their spouse or children or for a friend who sponsored part of the cost for them to go on the trip.

While in Ecuador, we went on such a trip and visited several small, nearby towns outside of Quito. A fascinating aspect of each of these small towns is that each is famous for a certain product. We often found 15-25 shops specializing in different variations of that same type of product on the same street in that town.

The first town we visited is a leather town. The fresh leather scent greeted us as we stepped off the bus. Over a hundred shops specialize in leather goods. Everything imaginable was in stock. Each store had a greeter at the door, inviting us to enter and look around. Boots, belts, purses, jackets, and beautifully crafted shoes of all sizes were lined up on tables, shelves, windows, and open closets. There were wallets, money belts, and much more.

All these leather goods were beautifully crafted by skillful local craftsmen.

They are quite a bargain if bought locally. However, more goods are made than can be sold locally, so they ship all over South America, where these same products are then sold for much higher prices.

The next town is noted for its woven textiles, hand woven with techniques handed down from father to son for many generations. As we watched the weavers, we developed an admiration for the bright colors, and the precise patterns used on the blankets, tapestries, shawls, and dresses.

Bartering is customary, and the sellers are disappointed if the tourists don't even try to barter. They always smile and say, "This is a special price, just for you."

Our third village is noted for its bread dough, handicrafts, and figurines. Traditionally, families light candles and put figurines on the graves of the family members on their Day of the Dead in November.

The figurines are usually dressed in indigenous costumes. Nativity and Christmas ornaments are abundant, as are magnets and other tourist trinkets.

The fourth town we visited was famous for its copper products. It also had strolling native musicians serenading us with their Andean pipe music. We have never seen so many copper products. They were simply amazing.

Our next village is well known for its ceramic pottery and various other items. I don't know who thinks up all these ingenious uses for ceramics.

Our last town is well known for its bizocos--flaky pastries, delicious to the taste, that just melts in one's mouth. Their aroma greets us as we disembark the bus.

Eaten while enjoying some cafe con leche (coffee with milk), this is quite a memorable treat. For a few bucks, a large sack full of these tasty pastries can be purchased and eaten on the bus.

By this time, all the men on the trip will be dragging in weariness, even though the women will still be eager to shop some more. Fortunately, the ladies took pity on us and relented They gave in, and we headed home.

**

Along with various shops, there will also be strange, rustic music, which has a haunting, unforgettable melody. A sidewalk café may be next in line. Sidewalk cafés can be quite cozy and really inviting. These are great places to sit down briefly for a cool drink in the shade and watch the people go by. The menu is usually simple but tasty, and at night they serve fancy dinners. The waiters are wonderful and helpful. Most people make a mental note to return the following year.

**

As we returned from driving through village after village, we realized that we were surrounded by the peaks of many tall volcanoes.

**

I have been in the Morelia, Mexico area several times, and we learned that many of their villages specialize in a product like this and are famous for this product.

**

One village is nicknamed Strawtown, because it concentrates on straw products. Another village is dubbed Silver city because it specializes in silver products.

Cruise lines often offer both a pre-cruise three-day package and/or a post-cruise three-day package, during which time one can see or do other things in that area. Some people take advantage of this opportunity after a mission trip, and on their own schedule a side trip afterwards and save on airfare.

**

Often the closing highlight of a trip is for the team, on the last night of the trip , to take their in-country coordinator with all the translators and other key personnel to a nice restaurant and recognize them for the help they have been. They enjoy this very much, and the recognition we give them, and it also encourages them to act as translators and workers on another trip.

Translators

On many of my mission trips, I have given a sermon or talk to various-sized groups, and-- of course--I have worked with a number of translators. A problem arises if one's translator only gives a literal translation of his words.

Frequently, we Americans use slang words unconsciously, and the faces of the audience will go blank in confusion if given a literal translation. If the translator has learned English from an Englishman, probably he will not understand our American slang and idioms.

One of the best translators I ever had was Pastor Negash Bedado from Addis Ababa, Ethiopia. He was fluent in both languages, he had been to America several times, and he understood our slang and gestures. Some people do a lot of gesturing and talking with their hands. When I gestured, he did too, but more emphatically.

When the tone of my voice rose, his voice rose even more. He was a gifted speaker.

The eyes of the people in the audience switched back and forth between the two of us, as we spoke, he translating each phrase or sentence after I spoke.

Personally, I think he gave a better sermon than I did. People nodded their heads in agreement, as he embellished on the stories that I told. His translation of the humorous illustrations I gave must have been supreme, because the audience laughed contagiously.

He not only translated what I said, he translated all of me, my words, gestures, laughter, facial expressions, everything. He was very good. I wished I had him all the time, and I told him so.

**

Chapter 23: Training to Share

Several years ago, the Billy Graham Association designed a new evangelism course, FM419, for upcoming crusades/ festivals. Young men and women need to be taught new ways of sharing, with others, the Good news about Jesus Christ.

Several thousand attendees took this new course. Hundreds made decisions for Christ. Basically this course teaches a student how to overcome his/her fear of sharing and his/her fear of rejection. Those finishing the course were challenged to be crusade/festival counselors.

Often, when people reject one's message about Jesus, they are rejecting Jesus, not the person delivering the message.

Anyone who is planning a mission trip or who is interested in better equipping missionary team members should consider ordering this FM419 course.

Another time-proven training plan is "Evangelism Explosion."

That is the purpose of all mission trips.

Chapter 24: Missionary Flights International

Behind the Scenes in Mission Support

When an author writes a book, there are many other unseen people who work behind the scenes: those who proofread, illustrate, make suggestions, write a chapter on a special interest subject, revise,...etc.

When Wycliffe Bible Translators are working, they need support and personnel to do electrical, plumbing, painting, carpentry repairs, computer repairs, auto repairs, office work,...etc. They are needed so that the translators are not interrupted from their translating work to do this vital work at the office or for their homes. In that way, the behind-the-scenes helpers speed up the translation work.

Likewise, when a missionary family or group goes out on the mission field, it needs help and support. Missionary Flights International (MFI) is a perfect example of that. MFI's mission is to glorify God by standing in the gap for over 700 Bible centered missionary families, missions, and churches within the West Indies (mostly to Haiti, Dominican Republic, and the Bahamas.) MFI is located in Ft. Pierce, FL.

The unseen crew of each flight are the staff of MFI aircraft mechanics who perform the maintenance that keep MFI planes airworthy. MFI's director of maintenance is a highly experienced mechanic and a designated FAA inspector, who can assure each passenger that every precaution has been taken to insure the airworthiness of MFI aircraft.

MFI airlifts passengers and cargo by maintaining scheduled passenger service each week to and from Haiti. Mission personnel such as families, medical teams, and work teams are airlifted at a substantial savings of time and airfare costs.

Mission cargo is received daily at the MFI hangar and is checked in by computer. The scheduled cargo flights each week expedite mission cargo within a few days of the date it is received. MFI provides the special handling and care that vital supplies and equipment require to assure safe arrival on the field.

MFI handles the first class mail and parcel post for all affiliated missionaries and missions. Mission mail is received daily through MFI's mailing address, is sorted and put in the various mission bags, and is loaded aboard each MFI flight. Affiliated missions also send back their U.S. stamped outgoing mail on MFI scheduled flights.

MFI serves as purchasing agent for missionaries in countries where few commodities are readily available. Purchase orders are sent to MFI via the mission mail. MFI locates a source, purchases the order, and schedules it out on the next available cargo flight.

The hallmark of MFI from the beginning has been to "stand in the gap" wherever we find it (Ezekiel 22:30). MFI continues to add services as they find areas of need among the missions they serve.

MFI has three DC3 planes and another DC3 on order to be delivered in a few months. MFI also has three small Cessnas for short trips. Each DC3 can seat up to 28 passengers.

Following the January 2010 earthquake in Haiti, MFI mobilized immediately and had planes going out the next day. Tons of relief supplies poured in from all over. Forty to a hundred volunteer workers arrived every day to help sort out the relief supplies and load the planes. Several other business companies loaned their large company planes and crew to MFI to be used for relief flights. The congestion of planes in Haiti was quite confusing.

MFI carried many work teams and medical teams to Haiti during this crisis.

After five or six months, the frantic, hectic pace of donated earthquake relief supplies and work has slowed down to a manageable level, and the need for so many extra workers is past. Praise the Lord! Now MFI is back to a normal workload. MFI accomplished miracles during this disaster.

To summarize. MFI gives passenger service, cargo delivery, mail delivery, purchasing support, and hurricane and earthquake disaster relief. They really fill the gap. They have touched the world since 1964.

I have gone to Haiti eight times on MFI planes before the earthquake, and twice since it. I have helped load many planes since the earthquake. I know from experience how many long hours of hard work and sweat goes into loading planes with all that cargo and supplies, unknown work about which the public knows little.

Note: much of this MFI information has been gleaned from MFI brochures, with permission from their president, Dick Snook.

Chapter 25: In Conclusion

I'm sure that many of you have heard an interesting talk about missions and seen pictures taken on the mission field and wished (dreamed) that you were there..

I hope this book will thrill you and intrigue you and shorten the time between just imagining mission life, and experiencing a short term mission trip in true life.

Probably you can't change your work or occupation at this time in your life, but you can make your free time a lot more exciting.

Short time mission trips are designed for busy people. They match you up with others who share similar expectations, personalities and interests. You meet face-to-face with many people who have never heard of Jesus, or know very little about Him, and opens the door to discussions about Him in low pressure sittings. or atmosphere.

A short term mission trip is a week or two escape from the hustle and bustle of Main Street in your home town. Each day as you walk along on your trip, you will meet bikers walkers, shepherds with some sheep, mothers with babies wrapped in blankets on their backs, instead of pushing strollers, dogs walking their owners, shoppers and shop owners. All these people are dressed much differently than in your home town

Also, if it has been several years since your last short term mission trip, perhaps this book will refresh your memory and give you new insights about mission trips. Have you missed the thrill of helping someone receive the Lord, or the gratitude of people receiving a Bible or New Testament in their own language? Remember the gratitude of people for their medical care and medicines, ,the gratitude of people who are now pain free from dental problems, or the gratitude of people who can now see again. Remember how you helped them build or enlarge their church building? They thank you.

One can't help but wonder "WHAT   IF" you had gone on that mission trip. Its amazing what a difference a short term mission trip can make in your life, and in their lives!!

**

P.S. On the following page you will find a poem I wrote to my fiancee many years ago when I was courting her.   She found it recently. I married her several months later.
Please allow me to share it with you.
Thank you.

Chapter 26: Poem

MY GIRL
To A.V.S. by S.C.M.
(Written during our engagement)

This is a poem of a girl named Anna
And Spencer--a boy born in Indiana.
When she gave him the eye
'Twas the end of that poor Buckeye.
Although he never learned the tuba,
He certainly learned about Cuba.

One day he went to church
But was left quite in a lurch,
For he saw a cute little Miss
That he just couldn't wait to kiss.

At first there was quite a race
Between the fellows from the Air Base,
But setting such a stiff pace
To be in her warm embrace,
He soon won the race,
Which led to wedding lace.

She is such a pretty girl,
And her hair has many a curl.
To see her pretty smile,
He would drive many a mile.
And to kiss her pretty lips,
He has driven many trips.

I would love to spend all night
Holding her so very tight.
I would squeeze and hug with all my might.
She would be so happy with no lights in sight.
Her soft, sweet kisses taste just right.
I always hate to say goodnight.

To be with her, I'll always desire,
For her kisses are like fire.
And I can't be called a liar.
I would like to say that I hope to sire
For her some day a little growth
And to create a new Meckstroth.

When our kids number four,
Let's not try for any more.
Some say they're cheaper by the dozen,
But who wants ten dozen cousin?

Although I'm not so good at public speaking,
I'll try to set your heart tingling
By saying that I love you very much
And wish to stay within your touch.
For you're the one girl in a million
Who's worth more to me than a million.

The sound of your sweet Spanish voice
Has made you the girl of my choice.
And after many a tender caress,
I know I'll never love you less,
For looking into your deep, brown eyes
I'll never be telling you lies.

When I say I love you, I love you
And hope that you love me, too.
Although we got acquainted mighty fast,
I'm sure our marriage will always last.
Love, respect, and admiration has built
Something no stress can ever tilt.

Chapter 27: Questions and Answers

Q & A # 1

Q: I am shy and afraid to go on a short term mission trip, because I don't make friends easily, and no one else that I know is going on that trip. I've always dreamed of going to a foreign country, but I just can't get up the courage to go, without knowing anyone else on the trip. What can I do?

A: Are you afraid of being an outsider on the team? Don't worry. When you meet your teammates face to face for the first time, you will find that some of them are just as timid as you are. Once they see that you are a hardworking, congenial member of the team, you automatically become an insider on the team. Everybody has a job to do on the team. You do your job, and you're in. Roll up your sleeves and get to work. Consider it a privilege to work together so that others can experience God's power to change their lives.

Happily, as awkward as making new friends can be, when everyone on the trip has the same mutual interests, that serves as a good icebreaker. You expect (1) to serve the medical needs of the people of that country, (2) to tell them about the love Jesus Christ has for them, and (3) to give them Bibles and gospel literature in their own language. I think you will find what a pleasant surprise that will be in making friends. Sharing values and activities is all that counts.

In addition to liking and respecting each other, appreciating their resourcefulness, their patience and the calm way they solve problems, you will find that your teammates are pretty laid-back and friendly. Just what you wanted in your new friends. When someone asks you a question about something in your field of expertise, you will feel as if you really belong on that team. Soon you will bond into a close-knit family.

After the trip is over, you might say to yourself, "I intend to take inventory of my own life, since I now realize that my life hasn't been making me as happy as I would like to be. I hadn't realized how much was missing from my life. I'm happier now that I have been on this trip with my new friends, serving the Lord. I've been planting gospel seeds that will make a difference in other people's lives."

Q & A #2

Q: I'm married. My husband wants to go hiking and camping in the mountains on our vacation. I want to go to the beach and go shopping in the evenings. How can we solve this problem?

A: This is an age old question, one asked by many people. There are many possible answers.

An obvious answer is to go to Hawaii to a resort on the beach. Then you can spend a couple of days on the beach and shop at night. Then the next few days go hiking and exploring in the nearby mountains and see some volcanoes and waterfalls.

Perhaps that would be too expensive, though. Let's consider the problem more. Many vacations are taken for a variety of reasons: (1) to get a change in scenery, (2) to do or experience new things, (3) to meet new people, (4) to get a change in your daily routine (to stop running from errands to appointments to meetings all day long), (5) to see how the other half lives, and/or (6) to fulfill a long-time dream.

How about one of these alternatives: (1) go on a one-week mission trip, scheduled to go into a mountainous area of that country, (2) go to a country you would like to visit, or (3) if you speak a foreign language, go to a country that speaks that language.

Often the last day is scheduled for shopping at local shops or bazaars. If you are in the medical field or speak a foreign language, you would probably be welcome on most mission trips to such a country. Then you could experience most or all of the reasons mentioned previously as reasons people go on vacations.

Perhaps all the exciting mission experiences will offer you a new perspective and bring you back year after year.

If you are lucky enough to have two weeks of vacation time, then go on a one-week mission trip to a certain country, followed by a one-week vacation or tour of that country.
If done in advance, you can schedule your plane tickets accordingly, and save the cost of another roundtrip fare at a later date.

My wife and I used the above cost-saving method to add a post-trip addition to our Paraguay mission trip. After a very fruitful mission trip helping the people of Paraguay, the rest of our team flew home, but we flew on to Buenos Aires, Argentina. We spent four or five interesting days there, seeing the sights, before returning home from South America.

If you enjoy going on short term mission trips, you may have found the formula for the ultimate yearly summer vacation. Each year, the two of you can plan two short term mission trips each summer to two different places, and you can be on the road again to the far ends of the world.

Q & A #3

Q: My wife and I have been retired for two years now, and we are bored to tears. I have played all the golf I want to, gone fishing more times than I can remember, and we have been on several trips around the USA and to Europe. We don't seem to have a purpose in life anymore. What can we do?

A: If you are a Christian, I would suggest that you and your wife go on a one week mission trip to some nearby country, or to a country you are interested in, and see what goes on. Help out in any way that you can. Watch what the mission team does and what the local pastors or missionaries do. See if you can help them.

Then go on a second mission trip to another country. Try to help in any way you can. Learn as much as you can about different aspects of life on the mission field. You say that you have gone fishing many times. Why don't you start fishing for souls?

Now that you know much more than before about life as a missionary, if you are still interested, contact the foreign mission board of your church and see if they need volunteers anywhere.

Another place to contact is Wycliffe Bible Translators. If you are the handyman type and can do a lot of the following, they would love to have you or any other volunteer workers who can do repair work, paint, lay bricks, do electric work, plumbing, car repairs, computer work, office work, repair washers or dryers, carpentry work,...etc.--basically almost anything. These volunteers are needed to keep the translators from having to take time off to do household repairs for their own families. Thus, the translation work is sped up. Fulfill your destiny.

God has an abundant and rich life for you to discover. Remember, retirement is not an interruption, but just a beginning in a new way to serve the Lord and follow his last commandment to go and preach the gospel to the ends of the world. Don't just keep the faith, share the faith.

Q & A #4

Q: We have no experience at all in organizing mission trips. How does our church go about organizing a successful medical mission trip to Peru, for example? What do we need to know and do?

A: First of all, it might be wise to ask the person from your church who conceived this idea of a medical mission trip for suggestions.

Next, I would advise you to phone another nearby church or organization that has organized at least two medical mission trips to that country recently, or to any other country. Tell them you need their advice for such a trip. If they are agreeable, make an appointment to go personally and see them and sit down and pick their brains for all the advice and details you can get.

If there are no nearby experienced groups that can help you, ask your pastor or contact your foreign mission board for information. If you still can't get the information you need, contact me, and I will give you some groups to contact.

If possible, have your prospective group leader go with another group on a similar trip someplace to become more knowledgeable and experienced about mission trips.

Most importantly, be sure you have a reliable, experienced in-country contact person who will make all the arrangements needed at his end. Give him a check-list of all the arrangements he needs to make. Keep in touch with him frequently. Call him 10 days before the trip and again the day before, and make sure he has everything covered.

If possible, it might be a good idea to collect all the passports ahead of time and give them to the team leader so that no one forgets to bring his passport. Sometimes that facilitates you getting a group check-in, which speeds up matters considerably.

Q & A #5

Q: Our church is planning its first ever mission trip, and we have calculated the cost for the trip and even allowed $2,000 for contingencies, and then divided the cost by the 20 members who expect to go. That amount seems to be higher than some of the prospective team members can afford. What can we do to reduce the cost?

A: An obvious answer is to have car washes, bake sales, garage sales, rummage sales,... etc. You could also have a mission-team fundraising walk. People get paid a certain amount for each mile they walk.

If possible, find a matching funds donor, who will match other people's donations up to a certain amount, and then find other donors who will have their donation doubled.

Some churches have a slave/servant sale, in which someone can purchase one of the team members for an hour or several hours to mow their yard, wash their car, rake the leaves, paint their garage, cook dinner for them, clean their house, clean out the garage, drive them to the store to go shopping, or any other such jobs around the house. The person is paid a set hourly rate, or job rate.

Other churches request each team member to turn in a list of 25 names and addresses of friends and relatives that they think might be interested in donating to the trip fund for them. The church prints out a nice letter telling about the trip and what the church hopes will be accomplished on the trip. Each team member receives an envelope with this letter, which he signs and mails. Each team member then sends a thank you letter to each person making a donation for him.

Another method often used is to find one or more benefactors with a heart for missions.
The total amount they donate towards this specific mission trip, is totaled together, and divided by the number going, which could lower the cost by $300-$500 per member.

There are many other possibilities.

If it is a medical mission trip, one way to save money, is to buy pills in bottles of 1000. We take these bottles to the country we visit, so that their Health Dept. or customs officials can see the expiration dates. Then when we arrive at our destination, we package and label the pills into standard dosages recommended by our MD's to eliminate counting in the pharmacy, since they are usually swamped.

Certain pharmaceutical or medical organizations can tell us what medicines are needed for each country or area. Sometimes they will ship us what we need for that area for a set price, which often is wholesale or even better.

Q & A #6

Q: My wife died about two years ago, and now I have recently been told that I have cancer and that I probably only have four or five years to live. Our children are all married, busy, and living in other states and doing fine. I am 67 and feel fine now. What can I do now?

A: Good advice for you would be to make sure that your will is up to date and that you have all your financial affairs arranged properly. You may want to consider leaving some of your money to your church.

Then ask your pastor for ways you can help at your church. People are always needed to visit the sick, or homebound, or in assisted living homes. Go on church visitation visits.
Learn to serve others. Don't sit at home feeling sorry for yourself.

Go on some short term mission trips. Experience firsthand the thrill of helping build a church for the needy, in some far away place. Enjoy using your own bare hands. Don't mind that you are sweating profusely as you do so. Help the sick on a medical mission trip. Many people / groups / tribes still need to hear the message of salvation.

Experience gratitude and smiles for all the medicine, glasses, and dental work given. See the thrill in these people's eyes when you give them a Bible in their own language.
Now you have a purpose in life, Keep doing this as long as you can.

Q & A #7

Q: How long does it take to plan a mission trip?

A: Probably 9-12 months, if you have never been to that place. If you have been there before and have a good in country contact person to work with, it can be done sooner, but it is always best to give yourself enough time and to allow for unexpected delays.

It takes a lot of planning and preparation for a short term international mission trip to a far-away country.

1. Your most important decision is to choose the most reliable in-country contact person you know to represent your team and make all your necessary arrangements there.
   Give him a list of things to do Check with him every couple of weeks. Then about a month before you leave, start checking every week, and during the last week, check every other day.

   Ask him if he has any suggestions on how to improve the trip. The success or failure of the trip hinges on these arrangements. Listen to his ideas.

2. Unless you can bring translators who speak the native language fluently, the people will not understand your group, and all your hard work and travel will be largely in vain.
   Perhaps your contact person can find enough good volunteer translators If not, hire enough experienced translators to meet your needs They are *so* very important.

3. There are some challenges when people from one culture work with people from different cultures, even when you are trying to spread the gospel.

   Read our newspapers, watch TV, for any news or current events about that country. Learn who their political leaders are and what type of government they have. Go to the library, to travel agents, or search the Internet to get information about the country, customs, exports, imports,...etc. Be sure of your sources.

Get a map of the country, learn about points of interest, famous spots and people,...etc.

4. Each member on the team should have several prayer partners here at home, praying for him every day. Also, pray that the hearts of the people you minister to will have receptive hearts. Pray for traveling mercies and for the safety of the team.

**